PREFACE

Are you an investor or entrepreneur looking to invest or start a business in any of the East African countries? Do you want to know the best investment opportunities or small business opportunities in East Africa for 2017? Then read on.

This book will show you clearly how and what to invest among the three countries, which are: Tanzania, Kenya and Uganda. All these countries' economies grow around 7% for the past ten years and still doing well. The United Republic of Tanzania is the second largest economy in the East African Community comprises of six countries and the twelfth largest in Africa.

The East African Community (EAC) offers excellent opportunities for new business ventures... East Africa is a region overflowing with potential – from agriculture to mining to tourism to energy – investment opportunities abound.

The book also provides the costs you will incur during registration and business set up. It shows you all the processes to pass through. The most interesting you are going to access online services to some of the procedures.

ACKNOWLEDGEMENT

I wish to thank all experts from various institutions who participated in designing and developing of this book in different capacities. I sincerely wish to acknowledge the contribution from the editors and proof reading specialists who struggled day and nights to make sure the book meets the international standard.

Specifically, i wish to thank MACP ONLINE BUSINESS institution for allowing their experts to participate in the development and prototyping of this book for validation process. It is through MACP ONLINE BUSINESS that most of the resources in this book came from. Their work to help authors in Tanzania reach their goals is the fundamental and progressive work to admit.

I also wish to recognize with appreciation the contribution of the above institution for allowing me to use the images and photographs from their resources. My gratitude to them goes beyond the thankful note.

Lastly, i would like to extend its sincere thanks to those who supervised this work.

Table of Contents

PREFACE 1
ACKNOWLEDGEMENT 2
Table of Contents 3
   CHAPTER ONE 4
   About Tanzania 4
   CHAPTER TWO 13
   Why Invest in Tanzania 13
   CHAPTER THREE 15
   Key Areas to Invest in Tanzania 15
   CHAPTER FOUR 32
   How to Invest in Tanzania 32
   CHAPTER FIVE 62
   About Kenya 62
   CHAPTER SIX 71
   The Reasons to Invest in Kenya 71
   CHAPTER SEVEN 75
   Potential Areas to Invest in Kenya 75
   CHAPTER EIGHT 83
   Procedures to Invest in Kenya 83
   CHAPTER NINE 114
   About Uganda 114
   CHAPTER TEN 122
   Why Invest in Uganda 122
   CHAPTER ELEVEN 124
   Business Opportunities in Uganda 124
   CHAPTER TWELVE 133
   Investing Procedures in Uganda 133
   References 144

CHAPTER ONE
ABOUT TANZANIA

The United Republic of Tanzania is located in Eastern Africa. It is bordered by Kenya and Uganda to the North, Rwanda, Burundi and the Democratic Republic of Congo to the West and Zambia, Malawi and Mozambique to the South. The country's eastern border lies in the Indian Ocean which has a coastline of 1,424 km.

Geography
Zanzibar is a part of the United Republic of Tanzania and consists of two main islands of Unguja and Pemba and a number of small islands. The Islands are located 40 km off the mainland coast of East Africa in the Indian Ocean. The two main islands are 40 kilometers apart, separated by 700 meters deep Pemba Channel.

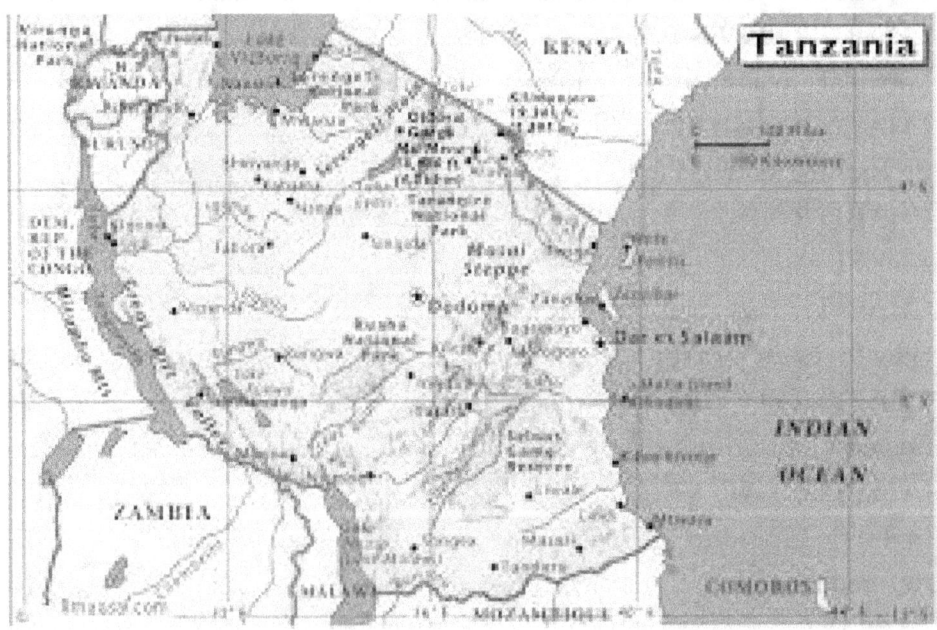

Area and Population

Tanzania has a total area is 945,087 sq.km including 61,000 sq. km of inland water. The total surface area of Zanzibar is 2,654 sq.km. Unguja, the larger of the two islands has an area of 1,666 sq.km, while Pemba has an area of 988 sq.km.

The 2012 Population and Housing Census (PHC) for the United Republic of Tanzania was carried out on the 26 th August, 2012. This was the fifth Census after the Union of Tanganyika and Zanzibar in 1964. The 2012 Population and Housing Census results show that, Tanzania has a population of 44,928,923 of which 43,625,354 is on Tanzania Mainland and 1,303,569 is in Tanzania Zanzibar.

Climate

Tanzania has a tropical type of climate and is divided into four main climatic zones notably: the hot humid coastal plain; the semi-arid zone of the central plateau; the high-moist lake regions; and the temperate highland areas. In the highlands, temperatures range between $10^{\circ}c$ and $20^{\circ}c$ during cold and hot seasons respectively. The rest of the country has temperatures usually not falling lower than $20^{\circ}c$. The hottest period spreads between November and February ($25^{\circ}c$ - $31^{\circ}c$) whereas the coldest period is often between May and August ($15^{\circ}c$ - $20^{\circ}c$).

The climate of the islands of Zanzibar is tropical and humid. Average maximum temperature is about $30^{\circ}C$ recorded during the hot season November to March, while average minimum temperature is $21^{\circ}C$, recorded during the cool season of June to October. Humidity rate is high ranging from 50's to 80's and slightly higher in Pemba than Unguja.

The Capital City

The official capital of Tanzania is Dodoma, which is located 309 km west of Dar es Salaam. Dar es Salaam is the country's commercial capital and is also the major seaport for the county's serving its landlocked neighbors.

Other big urban centres include Arusha, Moshi, Tanga, Mwanza, Morogoro, Mbeya, Iringa, Tabora, Kigoma, Shinyanga and Zanzibar.

Administrative Regions and Districts

The Government of the United Republic of Tanzania is composed of 30 administrative regions; 25 regions on the mainland and 5 in Zanzibar. Tanzania's regions are Arusha, Dar es Salaam, Dodoma, Geita, Iringa, Kagera,Katavi, Kigoma, Kilimanjaro, Lindi, Manyara, Mara, Mbeya, Morogoro , Mtwara , Mwanza, Njombe, Pemba North, Pemba South, Pwani, Rukwa, Ruvuma, Shinyanga, Simiyu, Singida, Tabora, Tanga, Zanzibar Central/South, Zanzibar North and Zanzibar Urban/West.

Culture

Tanzania has been described as one of the most diverse countries in Africa and this is reflected in the fact that there are more than 120 local languages spoken in the country. Swahili is the national language that is widely spoken while English is the official language of education; administration and business.

Local people are native African 99% (of which 95% are Bantu consisting of more than 120 tribes) and the remaining 1% consisting of Asians, Europeans, and Arabs.

Most of the population belongs to Christianity and Muslim religions though there is a small number of Hindus and atheists.

Generally, Tanzania culture is a product of African, Arab, European and Indian influences. Traditional African values are being consciously adapted to modern life, although at a much slower pace among the Maasai.

Politics

Since independence, Tanzania has been ruled by 4 Presidents, namely; the late Mwalimu Julius Kambarage Nyerere (1961-1985), H.E. Al Haj Ali Hassan Mwinyi (1985 – 1995); H.E. Benjamin William Mkapa (1995 –

2005). The current President of the United Republic of Tanzania is H.E. Jakaya Mrisho Kikwete (2005 to date).

The United Republic of Tanzania is a Democratic Republic. The Constitution of the United Republic of Tanzania guarantees political pluralism. Currently there are about eighteen (18) registered political parties. (http://www.nec.go.tz)

Since 1992, when the Multi-Party Political System was introduced in Tanzania, there have been three successful Presidential and Parliamentary elections. The first such election was conducted in 1995, followed by the 2000, and the 2005 elections.

Economy

Tanzania is a developing country and its economy depends heavily on agriculture. The sector accounts for more than 40% of GDP, provides 85% of the country's exports and employs 80% of the total workforce. Apart from the agricultural sector, tourism, mining and small scale industries are increasingly contributing to the national economic growth.

Currency

The Tanzanian shilling (Tsh.) is divided into 100 cents. Notes are in denomination of 500, 1000, 2,000, 5,000 and 10,000 shillings. Coins are in order of 5, 10, 20, 50, 100 and 200 shillings. Money can be changed in banks, Bureau de Change and other accredited points such as hotels. Credit cards (Access, Master Card, Visa, American Express, Euro Card and Diners) are accepted by major hotels around the country. Travelers' cheques in US dollars and Pound Sterling are recommended, although Euros are also accepted. Banking hours in major towns are from Monday to Friday (08.30 - 16.00 hrs), Saturday from 08.30 hrs - 13.30 hrs and are closed on Sundays. These may vary in smaller towns. ATM Machines are available in branches of major banks and accept most VISA cards.

HOW TO REACH TANZANIA

By Air

Tanzania is easily accessible by air, sea and road. With four international airports - Dar es Salaam International Airport (located 15 km southwest of Dar es Salaam and taking approximately 25 minutes to reach by car from the city center), Zanzibar International Airport (located approximately 7 km from the center and taking almost 15 minutes to reach by car, Kilimanjaro International Airport (40 km from Arusha town and takes almost one hour to reach by car) and Mwanza Airport that caters mainly for cargo uplifts especially of frozen fish fillet for the European Union market - travelers can easily plan their visits to Tanzania.

Major world airlines like British Airways, KLM Royal Dutch Airlines, Kenya Airways, Emirates, Ethiopian Airlines, Gulf Air, Air India, Egypt Air, South African Airways, Oman Air, Yemen Air and Qatar Airways fly in and out of Dar es Salaam , Kilimanjaro and Zanzibar International airports. Air Tanzania, Precision Air and a number of domestic commercial operators fly to various destinations within and out of the country.

KLM has daily non-stop flights from Amsterdam to Kilimanjaro and Dar es Salaam International Airports. Swiss International Airlines operates four weekly flights from Geneva and Zurich to Dar es Salaam. British Airways also operates three weekly non-stop from Heathrow to Dar es Salaam . Air India, Ethiopian Airlines, Kenya Airways, Egypt Air, Gulf Air, Emirates, Oman Air, Yemen Air and Qatar Airways link Tanzania with the Gulf, the Indian sub-continent and Far East, the People's Republic of China included.

By Railway

Tanzania is well served by two rail networks - the Tanzania Railways Corporation (TRC) which runs passenger and goods services along the central line between Dar es Salaam and terminal stations on both Lake Victoria (Mwanza) and Lake Tanganyika (Kigoma). Another link - Tanga Line, connects the northern coast port of Tanga with the northern regions of Kilimanjaro and Arusha.

The second rail network is the Tanzania Zambia Railway Authority (TAZARA). This line, which was financed with a historical generous grant from the People's Republic of China, runs southwest from Dar es Salaam for a distance of 1,800 km through the world's largest and famous Selous Game Reserve and the mineral rich southern highlands. It then runs across the border with Zambia and continues to New Kapiri Mposhi where it is well connected to the Democratic Republic of Congo, Zambia itself, Zimbabwe and South African Railway networks. Goods from Southern Africa utilize this railway by operating goods train services up to Kidatu where there is an Inland Rail Terminal liking with Tanzania Railways Corporation line.

By Road

Over 90% of passenger traffic and 80% of internal freight is carried by roads thus road network plays an important role in the socio-economic development of the country. The Tanzania National Roads Agency (TANROADS) is responsible for the management of the 35,000 kilometre trunk and regional roads network. The government, with the support of its development partners, has embarked on an extensive maintenance, rehabilitation and upgrading programme for all roads. The presence of Chinese construction engineers in this area is very conspicuous. Projects that have been completed include the construction of the longest bridge in Eastern, Central and Southern Africa - the Mkapa Bridge on Rufiji River along the Dar Es Salaam-Lindi-Mtwara Road and the 65-kilometre Wazo Hill-Bagamoyo road. The completion of these projects will improve living standards of people along their routes, improve access to areas of agricultural production and promote tourism.

By Sea/Lakes

There are four major ports: Tanga, Dar es Salaam, Mtwara and Zanzibar. These ports are well equipped and form a very important gateway link to the world and to the land-locked countries of Uganda, Rwanda , Burundi , the Democratic Republic of Congo, Zambia and Malawi . Several private ferry boat operators serve the Dar es Salaam - Zanzibar route using range of crafts from sailing dhows to tourist-class twin-hull fast boats. The fastest boat takes 75 minutes on a calm day. Bookings can be made
Useful Information before Travelling to Tanzania

Visa
Visitors are advised to have a valid visa before embarking on their journey to Tanzania. Visas can be acquired from any Tanzanian Embassy/High Commission, Consul General Office or Honorary Consul Offices.

Health

Visitors are advised to take precautionary measures to avoid being bitten by mosquitoes. Visitors may use insect repellent, wear long sleeved shirts and trousers in evenings and utilize mosquito nets. An International Certificate for vaccination against yellow fever is required to enter Zanzibar.

TRADE IN TANZANIA

Tanzania attaches great importance to the role of trade in realizing National goals on poverty eradication through structural transformation of the economy with the private sector taking a leading role as an engine for national economic growth.

Tanzania offers a well-balanced and competitive package of fiscal trade incentives especially in the priority sectors such as manufacturing, agriculture, Tourism, petroleum, gas and Mining. For all these sectors, except petroleum and gas sectors, acquisition of all capital goods and parts are zero rated for import duty purposes and VAT thereon deferred.

Research expenses for agriculture are allowable for income tax purposes, while capital acquisitions are 100% expensed. You can also import duty-free all capital goods, spare parts, hotel facilities, explosive material for gas and oil exploration. Tanzania has also signed double taxation treaties with Denmark, India, Italy, Norway, Sweden, Kenya, Uganda, Zambia and Finland.

Import products
Major import commodities include agricultural machinery, implement and pesticides, industrial raw materials, machinery and transportation equipment, petroleum and petroleum products, construction materials, consumer goods. The list is not exhaustive,

Export products
The principal export commodities include Minerals (gold, gemstones, diamonds, coal e.t.c.), coffee, cotton, cashew nuts, tea, sisal, tobacco, pyrethrum and cloves. The main imports are machinery and transport equipments, textiles and clothing, petroleum products.

Trading Partners
Tanzania's major trading partners include: China, Germany, Japan, India, the European Union, United Arabic Emirates, United Kingdom, Kenya, Japan, India and South Africa.

Major commercial/trading cities include Dar es Salaam, Mwanza, Zanzibar, Arusha, Mbeya, Tanga, Kilimanjaro and Kigoma.

CHAPTER TWO
WHY INVEST IN TANZANIA

Tanzania enjoys an abundance of natural wealth, which offers tremendous investment opportunities for investors. These include an excellent geographical location (six land locked countries depend on Tanzania ports as their cheapest entry and exit ports); arable land; world renowned tourist attractions (Serengeti, Kilimanjaro, Ngorongoro, and the Spice islands of Zanzibar); natural resources; a sizeable domestic and sub regional market; a wide local raw materials supply base; abundant and inexpensive skills; assurance of personal safety; warm friendly people and a suitable market policy orientation.

The following are among the major reasons why you should invest in Tanzania:

High degree of investment security because of unparalleled political stability that is strife-free without ethnic division; democratic rule that respects diversity of opinion and a strong tradition of constitutionality and rule of law;

Business-friendly Macro-Economic Stability with low inflation (4.2%), stable exchange rates supported by unrestricted and unconditional transferability of profits, loan repayments, emoluments, royalties, fees and changes;

Simplified bureaucracy, streamlined through the acclaimed services of the Tanzania Investment Centre which is a one-stop-facilitation agency of government serving registered investors and businesses;

Successful economic liberalization measures commended by both the World Bank and the IMF with business-supportive legislation continually being improved through genuine dialogue between government and the private sector

A well-balanced package of incentives to investors with additional negotiated benefits to strategic investors

Rapidly emerging as the most effective entry point and gateway for trade into Eastern, Southern and Central Africa; FAVOURABLE GEOGRAPHICAL LOCATION OF TANZANIA

Lucrative investment opportunities in infrastructure, privatization and value adding facilities.

Investment guarantees, and settlement of Disputes. Investments in Tanzania are guaranteed against Political risks, Nationalization and Expropriation.

Any foreign business operating in Tanzania may obtain credit from domestic financial institutions up to the limits established by the Bank of Tanzania. Major banks like Standard Chartered, ABSA, Barclays, Citibank, Stanbic, Exim etc. have invested in Tanzania.

Existing investors are ready to expand their businesses in Tanzania as depicted in the recent survey conducted by TIC, BoT and NBS.

Tanzania has been rated as number one investment destination with the highest sales growth by the UNIDO's Report of Foreign Investor Perception Survey, November 2003.

CHAPTER THREE
KEY AREAS TO INVEST IN TANZANIA

Opportunities for Investment in Tanzania

The Government of Tanzania (GOT) generally has a favorable attitude toward foreign direct investment (FDI) and has had considerable success in attracting FDI. In 2012, FDI into Tanzania rose to over USD 1.1 billion, the highest in East Africa. The legacy of socialist policies endures in certain sectors, however, and some officials remain suspicious of foreign investors and free competition. There are no laws or regulations that limit or prohibit foreign investment, participation, or control, and firms generally do not restrict foreign participation.

Agriculture

Agriculture has been destroyed by both internal and external factors. However, revival of the sector can provide European companies with a number of primary products desirable by their citizens and the world over. This is essentially coffee, cotton, tea, cashew nuts, cocoa, and vanilla. These products account for about 48 percent of Tanzania's GDP, provide 65 percent of total export earnings and are by far the largest employer. The sectors annual growth rate declined from 4% in 1999 to 3% in 2000 as a result of low short and main rainfall seasons, pests and inadequate availability and distribution of inputs.

The introduction of free market economy in 1985 has had a positive effect on the sector through introduction of semi-mechanized methods and new technologies especially in such sub sectors as cut flower and agro-processing industries. The growth of other sub sectors, e.g., agricultural equipment, farm implements, agricultural inputs is still characterized by import dependence. Investment in mechanized and intensive agriculture has not born fruits due to non-implementation of land law reforms that is expected to go hand in hand with the open economy. However, the government is in the final stage of submitting the land law reform bill to Parliament this year. It is expected that such reforms will attract more investors in agriculture.

In addition, the revival of agriculture is the only way to fill the pockets of majority of Tanzanians and hence increasing their purchasing power and demand for imported goods.

In terms of dynamic sub sectors in agriculture, the cut-flowers has had a multiplier effect in both imports and exports. The sub sector that was introduced some seven years ago has attracted investments in new technology on irrigation systems, greenhouses and refrigerated trucks. Kilimanjaro Airport Development Company (KADCO) which manages Kilimanjaro International Airport (KIA), the gateway for cut flowers in the north of the country has a plan for construction of cold storage facility for cut-flowers in year 2002.

The other contributors to the agricultural sector are fish especially Nile Perch in Lake Victoria that has attracted a number of fish filleting plants, "organic coffee" and pigeon peas in Arusha and Kilimanjaro regions that are being promoted by TechnoServe, as well as other non traditional crops.

In general, the agricultural sector offers European companies a big opportunity for technology investment in the areas of farm implements, agro-processing industries, agricultural machineries, irrigation equipment, fishing equipment, agricultural inputs as well as general commodity trading.

Information Technology

The IT sector has been the fastest growing sector in Tanzania for the past 10 years. The advent of the Internet has impacted growth across all sectors but notably in the accelerated growth of the computer market. In recognition of this phenomenon, the government removed duty on computers and peripherals in year 2000. The competitiveness of the market has widened the range of products on offer and lowered prices. All major brand names, Compaq, IBM, Apple, HP are represented by licensed distributors.

The Tanzania Telephone Company (TTCL) has been partly acquired by Dutch and German firms (MSI and Detecon). It has introduced new product lines and improved efficiency. There are four companies

(DATEL, WILKINS, SIMBANET, TTCL) that are licensed for data communication. In addition, there are four cell phone providers (Tigo, VodaCom, Zantel, Halotel and Airtel), five TV stations (ITV, TBC, CLOUDS, DTV, CTN, CEN) and 12 FM radio stations that offer a range of communication services to the public.

The IT sector, with its tremendous growth rate brings a big opportunity for business in Tanzania. The mushrooming number of Internet cafes in urban centers offers a big opportunity for computers, especially refurbished ones that are available in abundance in developed countries. In addition, most middle level managers and small businesses are taking advantage of the lower prices and are now computerizing offices and providing computer training in schools. This is potentially a big market for IT companies.

Environment and Energy

Tanzania has ratified several international and regional conventions with regard to environment regulations. However, like many developing countries, Tanzania is faced with fundamental environmental and energy challenges which have a big impact in the growth of the economy. Water pollution in coastal and inland waterways, industrial pollution in urban areas and de-forestations are the main environmental tyrannies facing Tanzania. Indeed, the country has not been able to take advantage of the available technologies to create a sustainable environmentally friendly situation The National Environment Management Council (NEMC) continues to offer technical assistance and raise awareness on rational resource use and environmental protection to government and general public.

Four management systems for assistance on adoption of environmentally sustainable natural resources management practices have been identified, namely: 1) the network of national parks, 2) the national system of game reserves as a second network of protected areas, 3) community-based approaches in areas adjacent to protected areas on lands owned by communities and supported by local districts and 4) coastal resources at both the national and local levels.

With regard to Energy, petrol fuel, hydro electric and coal are major sources of commercial energy in the country. Charcoal which results from tree burning are also widely used in urban areas with a very big price of environment degradation. The trend of energy consumption in Tanzania is dominated by biomass that accounts for 90%, petrol accounts for 8% and electricity accounts for 1.2%. Other energy sources such as coal, solar and wind accounts for less than 1%. The growth rate of the energy sector was 4% in 1999 and 5% in 2000 as a result of increase in production of electricity and demands by consumers particularly the industrial ones.

The opportunities available for the environment and energy sector are in the areas of: (i) petroleum-Tanzania Petroleum Development Corporation in collaboration with international companies, Dublin International, CANOP (T) Ltd and Ndovu Resources continue research and exploration in southern regions and along the coastal line (ii) solar - Global Environment Facility (GEF) sponsored data collection for preparation of solar development programme. Negotiations are in progress on reducing duties on solar equipment; (iii) natural gas - negotiations are ongoing on how to utilize natural gas found in deposits in the south coastal areas; (iv) wind: research on establishing speed of wind has been completed and potential areas are identified for wing energy and (v) geothermal on which research is ongoing and a private company, First Energy in collaboration with investors is working on possibility of starting an electricity generation project.

Health

The Health sector is faced by many challenges especially in the advent of HIV disease and immunity of chloroquine medicine to malaria. Statistics for 1996 to 1999 indicate that there has been little change in number of patients reporting and admitted in hospitals.

Malaria, AIDS, diarrhea and acute respiratory diseases are major causes and leading diseases for admissions and deaths. Medical services have been highly improved to ensure availability of drugs and essential medical equipment in hospitals and health centers. By year 2000, Tanzania had 179 hospitals, 529 health centers and 4005 dispensaries. In terms of ownership, government owned 60% of all health facilities, 20% was owned by the private sector, 15% by religious institutions and 5% by public institutions.

Tanzania imports almost 90% of its pharmaceuticals and medical equipment. Both imports and manufacturing of pharmaceuticals are regulated by the Tanzania Pharmacy Board. The three pharmaceutical manufacturing companies, Keko Pharmaceutical Industry, Shellys

Pharmaceutical Industries and Mansoor Daya Industries of Dar es Salaam are faced with cheap competing products mainly from India, China and other Far East countries.

Sales opportunities available in the health sector are in hospital equipment, research and production facilities, drugs and pharmaceuticals, preventive facilities e.g., condoms, mosquito nets, etc

Construction

The Tanzania Statistics Bureau does not keep data on construction activities in the economy. The available data is on construction of public works under the Ministry of Works. However, with the advent of the market economy, there are construction activities in the private sector that is not captured and could provide very significant information for income and job creation.

The Registration Board of Contractors registers contractors of various categories, monitors performance of contractors and building capacity in line with the current liberalized economical environment. The Board also registers and accredits engineers in the country while Tanzania Association of Consultants keeps a register of consultants. The two organizations provide a forum for construction issues. The National Construction Council is a regulatory body for civil engineering contractors. It approves the classification and registers/de-register contractors.

Tanzania recognizes that rural districts in Tanzania are the hub of agricultural production and home to 80% of the country's population. In view of that, the development objectives focus on a regional roads program down to the district level, which is responsible for supporting road maintenance to 60% of the country's roads. The objectives envisage, among other things, increasing the percentage of district roads rehabilitated/maintained by the private sector from 5% of all district roads (1997) to 80% in 2003. Additionally, over 1,000 Tanzanian contractors and consultants will receive both direct and indirect assistance in management and execution of road rehabilitation and road maintenance contracts.

The biggest opportunity available for the construction industry is in facilitation of importation of construction equipment for hire to small contractors. Small road contractors in Tanzania would benefit from the facility since they are unable to invest on equipment of their own.

Consumer Goods

Local industry accounts for some 15 percent of consumer goods used in Tanzania. It is mainly limited to the processing of agricultural products and light consumer goods. The gap of 85% is imported from South Africa, Kenya, the Middle East, India, the Far East (Singapore, Malaysia and South Korea, China, Japan and USA, UK countries). The increased trade, resulting from open market policy, has been well received but has also brought some concerns as some low quality products such as milk and milk products, fruit and fruit juices, toys, etc. from the international market are dumped in the Tanzanian market. The Tanzania Bureau of Standard has intervened and in some instances averted dumping of these products in Tanzania.

With a population of about 35 million, the slow pace of industrialization coupled with adoption of regional integration in East and sub-Saharan Africa, Tanzania's dependence on imported consumer goods is likely to remain for the coming 20 years or so. However, recent government effort in facilitating Export Processing Zones is expected to revamp the agro processing and increase agricultural goods for export and the internal market.

EAHP seeks to increase access to finance and improving management skills of the small and medium size sectors. It is expected that after provision of such services the small manufacturing enterprises will be able to contribute to the economy by increasing supply of goods.

Financial Services

Tanzania Finance and Enterprise Development (TFED) project (1993 –

1997) assisted the government of Tanzania to lay down a framework for reforms and ultimately liberalized the financial sector. Before 1995, public/state banks dominated the market. Interest rates were very high, investments were made with no basis for economic/financial viability, cost of borrowing was very high and lending to the private sector was limited to short term loan products.

Reforms of the financial sector exposed the public banks and the government to free market forces. Treasury Bills interest rates leveled to market rates, inefficient banks were closed or restructured while others were sold and acquired by efficient ventures and to top it all new local banks and foreign multinational banks entered the market. The list of banks operating in Tanzania is as shown below:

· Foreign banks:

(1) Citibank (USA) (2) Barclays Bank (UK) (3) Standard Chartered Bank (SA) (3) Amalgamated Bank of South Africa – bought National Bank of Commerce (4) Stanbic Bank (South Africa) (5) Kenya Commercial Bank (6) Malaysia Bank (7) Habib Bank (Pakistan) (8) East African Development Bank (9) United Bank of Africa (10) Euro Africa Bank

· National Banks:

(1) CRDB Bank (2) Akiba Commercial Bank (3) Tanzania Investment Bank (4) AZANIA Bankcorp (5) National Micro Finance Bank (6) CF Bank (7) EXIM (T) Bank (8) National Bureau de Change (9) Tanzania Postal Bank (10) Kilimanjaro Cooperative Bank and (11) 3 small community banks in Dar es Salaam, Mwanga and Mufindi

· Other Financial Institutions:

(1) Tanzania Development and Finance Limited (2) Capital Finance Ltd. (3) Fedha Fund Ltd (4) Savings and Finance Ltd

· Non Financial Institutions that offers some financial services:

(1) Social Action Trust Fund (SATF) – Seed fund of $ 10 million given by USAID to lend to large enterprises in private sector (2) Risk Management and Profit Sharing Fund (RMPS) – Seed Fund of $ 2 million given by USAID to lend to Small and Medium Enterprises (3) Mtaji Fund – Seed fund of $600,000 given by SNV – Netherlands (4) Small Enterprise

Loans Fund (SELF) – Seed Fund of $8 million loaned to government from ADF for lending to Micro Finance Institutions and about 12 NGOs that are donor funded.

The opportunities available for the sector are mainly linkage to sound investors as well as providing services to the growing number of community banks that require technology for efficient delivery of services. The biggest constraint for growth of commercial banks is savings mobilization as most banks are not yet able to serve the rural market. At present the commercial banks' network is limited to urban and peri-urban areas only. The lack of a development bank has been the biggest setback to financial institutions' contribution to the growth of economy as some sectors, e.g., agriculture, manufacturing, real estate, etc., requires long term loans that are not provided by commercial banks.

Mining

Though agriculture is the backbone of the economy, at present, mining is the engine of economic growth. The sector had a growth rate of 14% in year 2000 compared with 9% in previous year. During 2000 for example, income generated by mining sector increased 130% from $80.4 million in 1999 to $ 185.1 million. In 2000 Tanzania's mineral exports accounted to 27% of total exports. Production of gold and gemstones contributed to greater extent to the growth of the sector.

Gold mines are located in the northwest regions of Mwanza and Shinyanga as well as Mara region to the East of Lake Victoria. In year 2000 sales from gold export recorded an increase of 208% compared to 1999. Export sales of diamond from Williamson Diamonds at Mwadui recorded an increase of 70% from $ 43.75 million compared to $25.76 in 1999. Big international companies that are involved in mineral prospecting include Kahama Gold Mines Corporation, Ashanti Goldfields Limited, Resolute Limited, Afrika Mashariki Gold Mine,

Anglo – American Minerals, Tanganyika Gold Mines, Pangaea Minerals, Kiwira Coal Mines as well as Williamson Diamonds Limited.

In the year 2000, recorded production of gemstones was 151,000 kgs compared to 92,000 kgs in the previous year, an increase of 58%. Most of the gemstones are exported unprocessed thus fetching very low prices in the world markets. Gemstones that are abundant in the south, north and north east coast offer great potential, though full potential of the sub sector has not been realized. In the southern areas of Tanzania, at Tunduru and Songea districts, precious gemstones such as saphire, alexandrites, ruby etc are abundant in alluvial soils. Matombo Mountains and Mahenge areas in Morogoro region, are rich with deposits of ruby known all over the world as Matombo ruby. Areas of Tanga regions along Umba river are known by their potential for green garnets while the Arusha region at Mererani and Mbughuni produce the famous tanzanite, a rare ruby found in Tanzania only. Other gemstones that are found in the area includes rhodolite and tsavorite. Except for the tanzanite mining that has both mechanized and semi-mechanized production, mining of all other gemstones found in alluvial soils are controlled by approximately 50,000 small miners who uses hand tools and equipment. Actual statistics on contribution of gemstone to the economy are hard to find as a large part of the business is conducted outside official marketing channels. However, the government is now introducing regulation that will enable miners to disclose their transaction for verification and taxation.

Tanzania also boasts of deposits of coal, tin, phosphates, nickel, cobalt, copper, gypsum and pouzzolana. Exploration is ongoing to determine economic viability of large scale mining of the three minerals.
The opportunity for mining is in finding investors especially in locations e.g., Muheza and Chunya with gold deposits that lack a serious investor or venture partner who can collaborate with artisanal miners. As for small miners, the opportunity is on market linkage to international buyers as well as assistance on sourcing hand tools and small equipment such as water pumps, generators, compressors, etc.

Textiles

Tanzania produces raw cotton and textiles. Cotton is the fifth largest agricultural export commodity contributing 3% of total exports in 2000 after coffee (15%), raw cashew nut (9%), tobacco (7%) and tea (6%). However, the textile industry that was vibrant in the 1970's has lagged behind after market liberalization. This situation forced the government to sell ginneries and textile industries that were previously under public ownership and management in order to revamp the sector. As a result, Urafiki, Ubungo, Mwanza and Musoma textiles industries are all under new ownership. Production of textile was 74,000 sq. metres in 2000 compared with 50,000 sq.m. in 1999; an increase of 48%.

Private textile industries such as Sunflag and A-T Textiles (located in Arusha) as well as KTM of Dar es Salaam have been operating efficiently and currently are the largest contributor to the growth of the textile sector. Two of the companies have since been able to take advantage of the African Growth Opportunity Act (AGOA) and have started shipping textile products to USA this year.

The opportunities available in the textile sector are related to the AGOA and the capitalization process that will be undertaken by the private owners. The latter is envisaged to result to demand for linkage to suppliers of technology.

Tourism

Tourism is one of Tanzania's dynamic sectors that has shown significant growth in recent years. Tanzania's tourism policy that favours "selective" to "mass" tourism mainly for purposes of ecology conservation has in a way resulted to limited earnings albeit with a sound economic purpose.

Revenue from tourism increased a paltry 0.8% in the year 2000 compared to the previous year.

Tanzania has a wide range of tourist attractions with a potential for the best tourism industry in Africa. The Serengeti and Ngorongoro national park, with the crater in the rift valley, provides sanctuary to millions of animal species that attract tourists from the world over. The Selous National Park, the largest national park in the Africa is only surpassed by Serengeti for concentration of wild animals. Selous is a beautiful park used for eco tourism and bird watching. Mount Kilimanjaro, the tallest point in Africa, is a world attraction offering mountain climbing tourism. Other national parks like Mikumi, Manyara, Sadani, Katavi are all good tourist attractions. The Island of Zanzibar and the whole coastal area of the mainland have beaches of world class. Zanzibar itself has a wide coastal area for scuba diving that attracts tourists from all over the world. Cultural tourism centers have been established in Arusha, Kilimanjaro, Tanga and Mbeya regions.

Opportunities available in the tourism sector are agency services, camping equipment, vehicles, hotel equipment, diving equipment, tourist boats, mountain climbing equipment as well as tour promotion services e.g., web designing etc

Transportation

Tanzania's position on the world map makes it an obvious operator of land, marine and air transportation modes. Tanzania has 85,000 kms of roads out of which 13,630 are tarmac roads and 30,000 kms of rural roads. Tanzania also has 4,460 kms of two railway lines systems one running from Dar es Salaam to Mwanza, with a junction to Kigoma, Arusha and Tanga and another exclusively running from Dar es Salaam to Zambia. On waterways, Tanzania has a fleet of vessels in the inland waterways in lakes Victoria, Tanganyika and Nyasa and coastal shipping services. The country has four major costal ports at Dar es Salaam, Tanga, Mtwara and Zanzibar. In addition, the country has two international airports at Dar es Salaam and Kilimanjaro, and a number of other small airport and air strips.

All roads are under the authority of Tanzania Road Agency (TANROADS) that was given a mandate to operate a Road Fund for construction and maintenance of main roads and rural roads. Urban roads are under local government authorities. Road transportation services are provided almost entirely by the private sector with a higher growth rate than others. The Tanzania Railways Corporation (TRC) - undergoing privatization - and Tanzania Zambia Railways Authority operate railway lines with TRC operating the 2,600 km meter gauge railway that was owned by the former East African Railways and TAZARA operating 1,860 kms of standard gauge railways running from Dar es Salaam to Kapiri Mposhi in Zambia. The harbors are operated by the Tanzania Harbors Authority (under privatization). Air transport services are provided by both the public and private sector. However, the Air Tanzania Corporation (ATC) – national flag carrier airline is in the process of being sold to private operators.

The sector brings a big potential for European companies especially in the area of inland cargo transportation equipment for road services and marine transportation in both inland and coastal waterways. Other available opportunities are in passenger transportation equipment, small and medium air transportation equipment as well as traffic monitoring equipment.

CHAPTER FOUR
HOW TO INVEST IN TANZANIA

STARTING A BUSINESS

Tanzanian businesses can be registered as a business name, a local company or a foreign company.

Business Registrations and Licensing Agency (BRELA) is responsible for business registration in Tanzania. BRELA issues certificates of compliance for foreign companies, certificates of incorporation for local companies and certificates of registration for single proprietorship. Firms must then register their businesses with the Tanzania Revenue Authority (TRA), the National Social Security Fund (NSSF) or any of the other five social security schemes in Tanzania and, depending on their business activities; they should obtain licenses with the Ministry of Industry and Trade or the Municipality.

THE COMPANY YOU MAY OPEN IN TANZANIA

STARTING A LOCAL COMPANY

TYPE A COMPANY

Type 'A' companies obtain their business license from the Ministry of Industry and Trade. See what category your business falls into.

Type A companies

- Estate agent, Estate developer, Property management, Real estate agent
- Shipping agent
- Shipping business
- Commercial traveler
- Clearing and forwarding /freight forwarders
- Insurance and assurance, insurance broker, Re-insurance
- Tourist Hotels, lodges, camps, Tour operators, Hunting Safaris, Travel agent, Car hiring and
renting, Tourist photographic and Tourist promotion
- Banking and Financial institutions, Capital markets and Credit card management, stock
exchange and stock exchange brokers
- Transportation of passenger or goods by air
- Postal services
- Transportation of passenger or goods by railway
- Fax, Telex, email, internet service providers, Internet café, internet surfing, Telecommunications service and sales of telecommunication equipment
- Cargo valuation, cargo superintendence and pre-shipment inspection
- Cargo tallying
- Harbours and cargo handling
- Electricity production and distribution
- Bureau de Change

- Stevedoring or lighter age
- Courier services and mail agent
- Broadcasting and television
- Ship chandlers/ miscellaneous port services
- Refining crude oil
- Night clubs
- Dealers in arms and ammunition
- Dealers in explosive
- Social security provider
- Export and selling
- Water drilling and supply
- Dealers in broadcasting apparatus
- Manufacturing and selling
- Motor vehicles and dealers
- Commission agent or Manufacture's representatives
- Import and selling
- Gold and silver smith and Gemstone dealers
- Any business of international nature governed by policy

TYPE B COMPANY

Type 'B' companies obtain their business license from the Municipality where the business premises are located. See what category your business falls into.

Type B companies
- Insurance agent
- Restaurant and ordinary hotels and guest houses
- Auctioneers
- Itinerant trade
- Supermarkets, departmental stores etc
- Regional Trading companies
- Cooperative societies
- Wholesale trade

- Building contractors, electrical contractors, mechanical contractors, civil works contractors, etc
- Specified professionals
- Printing and publishing of books and newspapers
- Spare parts and machine tools
- Broker
- Transportation of passengers within the city, Municipal and township
- Small scale manufacturing and selling
- Attended telephone services
- Any other business which is not of national/ international nature or not governed/ proceeded by policy

REGISTER A COMPANY ONLINE

PROCEDURES
1. OBTAIN NOTARIZED DOCUMENTS

Requirements
1. Memorandum and Articles of association (original)
2. Lease agreement (original)
3. Physical presence
of one of the shareholders of the company to be formed or their authorized representatives
4. Passport (Simple copy) of all shareholders

In addition, for an authorized representative
1. Power of attorney (an authentic copy)

COSTS
Cost detail
Notarization fee for Memorandum and Articles of association
TZS 10,000

Notarization fee for lease agreement
TZS 10,000
Notarization fee for Declaration of compliance form form14b
TZS 10,000
Payment methods: cash

As time i am writing this book, exchange rate was as follows:
1 Tanzanian Shilling = 0.00044903 American Dollar
(Updated 18:00:00(EAT) 17/04/2017)
Source: https://fx-rate.net/TZS/USD/
Time frame
Waiting time in queue: Max. 5mn
Attention at counter: Min. 5mn - Max. 10mn

Additional information
It is mandatory to notarize the articles and memorandum of association for authentication before submitting them to Business Registration Licensing Authority(BRELA).

2. APPLY FOR COMPANY REGISTRATION

Apply online here: http://tiw.tic.co.tz/
Requirements
1. Notarized memorandum and articles of association (2 original)
2. Notarized lease agreement (Simple copy)
or Title deed (Simple copy) for business premises
3. Passport (Simple copy) for each shareholder

COST
For all companies
TZS 500,000
for business license - average business license cost for domestically owned company

TZS 45,000
for filing fees for memorandum and articles of association and company registration form

TZS 5,000
stamp duty for registration of memorandum and articles of associations

10 % - TZS 0
of the total cost as facilitation fee

For companies with capital
TZS 50,000
registration fee if nominal share capital is inferior or equal to Tshs.500,000

or TZS 80,000
if nominal share capital is more than Tshs.500,000 but not more than Tshs.1,000,00

or TZS 100,000
if nominal share capital is more than Tshs.1,000,000 but not more than Tshs.2,000,000

or TZS 120,000
if nominal share capital is more than Tshs.2,000,000/= but not more than Tshs.3,000,000

or TZS 150,000
if nominal share capital is more than Tshs.3,000,000/= but not more than Tshs.5,000,000
or TZS 180,000
if nominal share capital is more than Tshs.5,000,000/= but not more than Tshs.10,000,000

or TZS 200,000
if nominal share capital is more than Tshs.10,000,000/= but not more than Tshs.30,000,000

or TZS 300,000
if nominal share capital is more than Tshs.30,000,000/= Registration fee for companies not having share capital

For companies with no capital
or TZS 50,000
f number of members as stated in the Articles of Association does not exceed 25

or TZS 60,000
if number of members as stated in the Articles of Association exceeds 25 but does not exceed 50

or -1 70,000
if number of members as stated in the Articles of Association exceeds 50 but does not exceed 100

or -1 80,000
if number of members as stated in the Articles of Association exceeds 100 but does not exceed 150

or TZS 90,000
if number of members as stated in the Articles of Association exceeds 150 but does not exceed 200

or TZS 120,000
if number of members as stated in the Articles of Association exceeds 200

Time frame
Waiting time until next step: Min. 5 days - Max. 10 days

As time i am writing this book, exchange rate was as follows:
1 Tanzanian Shilling = 0.00044903 American Dollar
(Updated 18:00:00(EAT) 17/04/2017)
Source: https://fx-rate.net/TZS/USD/

3. BIO-METRIC FINGER PRINT AND PHOTO SHOOT

Requirements
1. Physical presence of the applicant
2. Passport (original)

Time frame
Waiting time in queue: Min. 5mn - Max. 10mn
Attention at counter: Min. 5mn - Max. 10mn

4. OBTAIN COMPANY REGISTRATION CERTIFICATES

Requirements
1. Notarized memorandum and articles of association (2 simple copies)
2. Notarized lease agreement (Simple copy)
3. Title deed (Simple copy)
4. Passport (original) of each shareholder

Note:
Obtain a business license

5. ASSESSMENT OF DOCUMENTS AND FEES

Requirements
1. Business license application form (original)

2. Certificate of incorporation (Simple copy)
3. Tax Identification Number (TIN) (Simple copy)
or Resident permit class "A" (Simple copy)
Showing the holder to be investor in that company / business.
4. Notarized lease agreement (Simple copy)
or Title deed (Simple copy)
5. Power of attorney (an authentic copy)
To a Tanzanian citizen or to a resident, in case the shareholders of the company are non-residents.

Additional requirements for specific businesses
1. Customs Agency license (Simple copy) for those applying for clearing and forwarding licenses.
2. Tourism Agency license (Simple copy) for those applying for licenses related to tourism promotion.
3. Professional certificates (Simple copy)
For all professional businesses (Dispensaries, Consultancies, Advocates, Pilots, Ship Captains, etc.)
4. Air worthiness Authorizing aircraft to fly.
5. Sea worthiness Authorizing ship to sail.

Time frame
Waiting time in queue: Max. 5mn
Attention at counter: Min. 5mn - Max. 10mn
Waiting time until next step: Min. 1 day - Max. 2 days

6. PAY LICENCING FEES

Requirements
1. Account number 0150259058700
2. CRDB bank slip (original)

COST

Cost detail

Agency business- Principal license fee
or TZS 300,000
business license for commission agent
or TZS 200,000
business licence for travel agent
or TZS 1,000,000
business license for shipping agent

Broker Business
or TZS 200,000
business license for local insurance
or USD 3,000
business license for foreign owned insurance broker
or TZS 1,000,000
business license for local shipping broker
or TZS 5,000
business license for foreign owned shipping broker

Payment methods: cash

Time frame
Waiting time in queue: Min. 15mn - Max. 30mn
Attention at counter: Max. 5mn

As time i am writing this book, exchange rate was as follows:
1 Tanzanian Shilling = 0.00044903 American Dollar
(Updated 18:00:00(EAT) 17/04/2017)
Source: https://fx-rate.net/TZS/USD/

7. SUBMIT BANK SLIP

Requirements
1. Bank slip 1 (original)

Time frame
Waiting time in queue: Max. 5mn
Attention at counter: Max. 5mn

8. OBTAIN A BUSINESS LICENCE

Requirements
1. Physical presence of the applicant
2. Passport (original)

Time frame
Waiting time in queue: Max. 5mn
Attention at counter: Min. 5mn - Max. 10mn

REGISTRATION OF FOREIGN COMPANY

A foreign company is a company that is registered/incorporated outside Tanzania. They may conduct business in Tanzania by opening a branch in Tanzania. In this case a foreign company can also be a company that has been incorporated in Tanzania but with majority shareholding (51%) being owned by a foreigner.

PROCEDURES
1. SUBMIT REQUEST AND OBTAIN NOTARIZED DOCUMENTS

Requirements
1. Return and declaration delivered form (form- 434) (original)
2. Lease agreement (Simple copy)

COST
Cost detail
TZS 10,000
notarization fee for form 434

Payment methods: cash
Time frame
Waiting time in queue: Min. 5mn - Max. 15mn
Attention at counter: Min. 5mn - Max. 10mn

Additional information

The user needs to certify memorandum and articles of association and the certificate of incorporation from their country of their origin or consult local embassy in Dar es Salaam. Users are advised to verify with Tanganyika Law society whether the lawyers they choose to notarize, certify documents or get any legal advices are still genuine and current

As time i am writing this book, exchange rate was as follows:
1 Tanzanian Shilling = 0.00044903 American Dollar
(Updated 18:00:00(EAT) 17/04/2017)
Source: https://fx-rate.net/TZS/USD/

2. ASSESSMENT OF DOCUMENTS AND FEES

Requirements
1. Notarized return and declaration delivered form (form 434) (original + an authentic copy)
2. Financial statements (Simple copy)
Most recent
3. Certified certificate of incorporation (Simple copy)
Certified as a true copy form the parent nation, or at the Embassies
4. Certified Memorandum and Articles of Association (Simple copy + an authentic copy)
Certified as a true copy form the parent nation, or at the Embassies

Time frame
Waiting time in queue: Max. 5mn
Attention at counter: Min. 5mn - Max. 10mn

Additional information
The number of Memorandum and Articles of Association brought to BRELA depends on the customer. If the Memorandum and Articles of

Association is not written in the English language, It should be translated to English and then certified as a true copy. Certification will take place at the parent nation or at one embassy.

3. PAY COMPLIANCE FEES

Requirements
1. Assessment form (original)

Costs
Cost detail

Registration fee
USD 750
For the registration of certified copy of a charter, statute or memorandum and articles of the company, or other instrument constituting or defining the constitution of the company
USD 220
For registration or filing any document required to be delivered to the Registrar under Part XII of the Act/other than the balance sheet

Filing Fees
USD 220
For filing of Balance Sheet
USD 25
For late filing/registration fee to be paid to the Registrar of any document delivered to him out of time per month or part thereof

Payment methods: cash, check

Time frame
Waiting time in queue: Min. 5mn - Max. 15mn
Attention at counter: Min. 5mn - Max. 10mn

Additional information

A bank slip must be issued for all payment to the Registrar of companies. Any request of money which is not within the payment schedule stated should be reported through phone call to: +255 218 0113, +255 218 1344 or +255 218 0141

The total fee payable includes three fees i.e the registration fee which depends on a company's nominal share capital, filling fee and Stamp Duty

As time i am writing this book, exchange rate was as follows:
1 Tanzanian Shilling = 0.00044903 American Dollar
(Updated 18:00:00(EAT) 17/04/2017)
Source: https://fx-rate.net/TZS/USD/

4. SUBMIT REQUEST FOR COMPANY REGISTRATION

Requirements
1. Notarized return and declaration delivered form (form 434) (original + an authentic copy)
Filled, stamped & signed by one of the directors
2. Certified Memorandum and Articles of Association (Simple copy)
Certified as a true copy form the parent nation, or at the Embassies
3. Certified certificate of incorporation (Simple copy)
Certified as a true copy form the parent nation, or at the Embassies
4. Financial statements (Simple copy)
5. CRDB payment Slip (original)

Time frame
Waiting time in queue: Max. 10mn
Attention at counter: Max. 5mn
Waiting time until next step: Min. 1 day - Max. 3 days

Additional information
A receipt must be issued for all payment to the Registrar of companies. Any request of money which is not within the payment schedule stated should be reported through phone call to: +255 218 0113, +255 218 1344 or +255 218 0141

5. OBTAIN CERTIFICATE OF COMPLIANCE

Requirements
1. Payment receipt (BRELA - company) (original)

Time frame
Waiting time in queue: Min. 5mn - Max. 10mn
Attention at counter: Max. 5mn

Additional information
Foreign companies are required to file only audited balance sheets of their companies.

6. SUBMIT LEASE AGREEMENT DOCUMENTS

Requirements
1. Notarized lease agreement (original)
2. Lease and property registration form (LR 66 form) (2 original)
3. Passport (original) copy

Lease agreements with contract terms above 5 years
1. Title deed (original) for endorsement
2. Passport (original)

Time frame
Waiting time in queue: Min. 10mn - Max. 20mn

Attention at counter: Max. 5mn

7. PAY REGISTRATION FEE AND STAMP DUTY

Requirements
1. Signed lease and property registration form (LR 66) (original)

COSTS
Cost detail

TZS 80,000
registration fees for a lease agreement of less than five years

or 50 % monthly rent - TZS 500
registration fees of a lease agreement exceeding 5 years
1,000
1 % yearly lease - TZS 120
stamp duty for lease registration
12,000

Payment methods: cash, Banker's check

Time frame
Waiting time in queue: Min. 10mn - Max. 15mn
Attention at counter: Max. 5mn
Waiting time until next step: Min. 7 days - Max. 15 days

As time i am writing this book, exchange rate was as follows:
1 Tanzanian Shilling = 0.00044903 American Dollar
(Updated 18:00:00(EAT) 17/04/2017)
Source: https://fx-rate.net/TZS/USD/

8. OBTAIN REGISTERED NOTARIZED LEASE AGREEMENT

Requirements
1. Signed lease and property registration form (LR 66) (original)

Time frame
Waiting time in queue: Min. 10mn - Max. 15mn
Attention at counter: Max. 5mn

9. SUBMIT REQUEST FOR TAX IDENTIFICATION NUMBER

Requirements
1. TIN application form (original)
2. Estimate of tax payable by installments form (original)
3. Registered lease agreement (Simple copy)
or Endorsed title deed (for contracts older than 5 years) (Simple copy)
4. Certificate of compliance (Simple copy)
5. Certified Memorandum and Articles of Association (Simple copy)

In addition, for each director
1. Shareholder TIN application form (original)
2. Passport (Simple copy) for each director

Time frame
Waiting time in queue: Min. 5mn - Max. 15mn
Attention at counter: Min. 5mn - Max. 10mn

Additional information
At least one director of the company must be physically present at the tax office to give their fingerprints. For any enquiry related to tax payment or complaints dial toll free 0800110016 for TTCL and Vodacom subscribers, 0786 800000 for Airtel and 0713800333 for Tigo subscribers

10. BIO-METRIC FINGER PRINT AND PHOTO SHOOT

Requirements
1. Physical presence
2. Passport (original)

Time frame
Waiting time in queue: Min. 20mn - Max. 30mn
Attention at counter: Max. 5mn
Waiting time until next step: Min. 1 day - Max. 3 days

11. OBTAIN TAX IDENTIFICATION NUMBER (TIN) AND TAX ASSESSMENT FORM

Requirements
1. Passport (original) in case of representative

Time frame
Waiting time in queue: Min. 5mn - Max. 10mn
Attention at counter: Min. 5mn - Max. 10mn

12. SUBMIT BUSINESS LICENCE REQUEST

Requirements
1. Business license application form (original)
2. Tax Identification Number (TIN) Certificate (Simple copy)
3. Certificate of compliance (Simple copy)
4. Certified Memorandum and Articles of Association (Simple copy)
5. Certified certificate of incorporation (Simple copy)
or Resident permit class "A" (Simple copy) Showing the holder to be investor in that company / business.
6. Power of attorney (an authentic copy)
To a Tanzanian citizen or to a resident, in case the shareholders of the

company are non-residents.

7. Proof of suitable business premises for the business applied for
This may be: copy of title deed, tenancy agreement; or receipt of rent or property payment.

Additional requirements for specific businesses
1. Customs Agency license (Simple copy)
For those applying for clearing and forwarding licenses.
2. Tourism Agency license (Simple copy)
For those applying for licenses related to tourism promotion.
3. Professional certificates (Simple copy)
For all professional businesses (Dispensaries, Pilots, Ship Captains, etc.)
4. Air worthiness Authorizing aircraft to fly.
5. Sea worthiness Authorizing ship to sail.

Time frame
Waiting time in queue: Max. 5mn
Attention at counter: Max. 5mn
Waiting time until next step: Max. 1 day

Additional information
Depending on the business activity, some companies will be required to obtain specific business licenses before obtaining a business licence from the ministry of industry and trade. Above are just few of the many specific licences a company could obtain.

13. PAY LICENCING FEES

Requirements
1. Account number 0150259058700

COSTS
Cost details

Agency business- Principal license fee

TZS 300,000
business license for commission agent
or TZS 200,000
business license for travel agent
or TZS 1,000,000
business license for shipping agent
Broker Business
or TZS 200,000
business license for local insurance
or USD 3,000
business license for foreign owned insurance broker
or TZS 1,000,000
business license for local shipping broker
or TZS 5,000
business license for foreign owned shipping broker

As time i am writing this book, exchange rate was as follows:
1 Tanzanian Shilling = 0.00044903 American Dollar
(Updated 18:00:00(EAT) 17/04/2017)
Source: https://fx-rate.net/TZS/USD/

Payment methods: cash

Time frame
Waiting time in queue: Min. 15mn - Max. 30mn
Attention at counter: Max. 5mn

Additional information
Above are just a few of the licensing fees, see the link for a list of all licensing fees http://www.tic.co.tz/media/Business%20license%20fees.pdf

14. OBTAIN RECEIPT

Requirements
1. CRDB bank slip (original)

Time frame
Waiting time in queue: Min. 5mn - Max. 10mn
Attention at counter: Max. 5mn

15. OBTAIN A BUSINESS LICENCE

Requirements
1. Physical presence of the applicant or a representative given that they will sign on the register book that they have taken on behalf of the applicant.

Time frame
Waiting time in queue: Max. 5mn
Attention at counter: Max. 5mn

16. SUBMIT REQUEST FOR VALUE TAX REGISTRATION

Requirements
1. Business license (Simple copy)
2. Application and registration form (VAT 101) (original)

Time frame
Waiting time in queue: Min. 10mn - Max. 15mn
Attention at counter: Min. 10mn - Max. 15mn
Waiting time until next step: Min. 1 day - Max. 2 days

Additional information
When submitting a request for VAT the tax officer is obliged to have a

short interview with the customer to establish eligibility of VAT Registration. The officer may request to inspect the business premises of the applicant. For any inquiry related to tax payment or complaints dial toll FREE 0800110016 for TTCL and Vodacom subscribers, 0786 800000 for Airtel and 0713800333 for Tigo subscribers

17. OBTAIN VAT CERTIFICATE

Time frame
Waiting time in queue: Min. 5mn - Max. 10mn
Attention at counter: Min. 5mn - Max. 10mn

Additional information
Advise to obtain an Electronic Fiscal Device (EFD) from a TRA EFD approved suppliers

18. SUBMIT REGISTRATION REQUEST

Requirements
1. Application for employer's registration (form R1) (3 original)
Three R1 forms need to be filled but only one is attached with the requirements
2. Business license - Ministry of Industry and Trade (Simple copy)
3. Tax Identification Number (TIN) Certificate (Simple copy)
4. Certificate of compliance (Simple copy)
5. Certified certificate of incorporation (Simple copy)
6. Passport

Time frame
Waiting time in queue: Min. 5mn - Max. 15mn
Attention at counter: Min. 5mn - Max. 10mn
Waiting time until next step: Min. 1 day - Max. 3 days

19. OBTAIN SOCIAL SECURITY NUMBER

Requirements
1. Passport (original)
of a person obtaining the social security number.

Time frame
Waiting time in queue: Max. 5mn
Attention at counter: Max. 5mn

Additional information
Form R2 (white) is the notification letter that an applicant (company) has been issued with social security number. R2 is attached with one R1 (yellow) form. The two R1 forms remain with NSSF for record purposes.

REGISTER A BUSINESS NAME

Registering a business name is the simplest way to start and conduct business in Tanzania. It is also the most inexpensive and easiest business form to maintain. In Tanzania individuals (sole proprietors) or partners (partnerships) who wish to register their business as personal business other than companies are categorized under Business Names.

Processing documents for business name registration

1. ASSESSMENT OF DOCUMENTS AND FEES

Requirements
For Individuals/ Sole Proprietors
1. Application form for registering a business name (form 3) (original)
For Firms/ Partnerships
1. Application form for registering a business name (form 2) (original)

Time frame
Waiting time in queue: Max. 5mn
Attention at counter: Min. 5mn - Max. 10mn

2. PAY BUSINESS NAME FEES

Requirements
1. Assessment form (original)

COSTS
Cost detail

TZS 5,000
Business name registration fee
TZS 1,000
maintenance fees paid manually

Payment methods: cash, check

Time frame
Waiting time in queue: Min. 5mn - Max. 15mn
Attention at counter: Min. 5mn - Max. 10mn
Waiting time until next step: Min. 1 day - Max. 3 days

As time i am writing this book, exchange rate was as follows:
1 Tanzanian Shilling = 0.00044903 American Dollar
(Updated 18:00:00(EAT) 17/04/2017)
Source: https://fx-rate.net/TZS/USD/

Additional information
A bank slip must be issued for all payment to the Registrar of companies. Any request of money which is not within the payment schedule stated should be reported through phone call to: +255 218 0113, +255 218 1344 or +255 218 0141

The total fee payable includes three fees i.e the registration fee which depends on a company's nominal share capital, filling fee and Stamp Duty

3. SUBMIT APPLICATION FORM FOR REGISTERING A BUSINESS NAME

Requirements
For Individuals/ Sole Proprietors
1. Application form for registering a business name (form 3) (original)
2. CRDB payment Slip (original) For Firms/ Partnerships
1. Application form for registering a business name (form 2) (original)
2. CRDB payment Slip (original)

Time frame
Waiting time in queue: Max. 5mn
Attention at counter: Min. 5mn - Max. 10mn

4. OBTAIN CERTIFICATE OF REGISTRATION OF BUSINESS NAME

Requirements
1. Payment receipt (original)

Time frame
Waiting time in queue: Max. 5mn
Attention at counter: Max. 10mn

LAND AND PROPERTY

According to the Land Act of 1999, all land shall continue to be public land and remain vested in the President as trustee for and on behalf of all the citizens of Tanzania.

The law recognizes three types of land in Tanzania namely General land, Village land and reserved land:

- General land is a surveyed land usually located in urban and

peri-urban centers.
- Village land is usually land in villages and within villages in rural Tanzania. Some village land has been surveyed but the majority of the land is un-surveyed. Village land cannot be used for investment until it is transferred into general land.
- Reserved land includes that reserved for forestry, National parks, public recreation grounds etc.

Obtain land (for Investors)

Foreign investors can obtain land for investment through Tanzania Investment Centre, where a "Derivative Right" is granted. There are two main ways by which investors can obtain land for investment:

1) To apply for land acquisition from the village, and then follow all the necessary steps required, until the land is transferred from village land to general land and given to TIC in order to prepare a Derivative Right for the investor.

2) To purchase a parcel of land from individuals/Companies; once the

buyer and a seller have agreed upon the price, the seller is required to surrender the land title to the Commissioner for Lands in order to re-issue in the name of TIC, which will eventually prepare a Derivative Right for an investor.

Obtain a construction permit
Construction permits are issued by the Municipal council in the municipality where the construction will take place.

IMMIGRATION AND LABOUR SERVICES

Any person who wishes to employ or engage a non-citizen in any occupation shall apply for a work permit to the labor Commissioner prior to the entry by that non-citizen. Work Permits are issued by Labour Commissioner. After obtaining work permit a non-citizen is required to apply for a resident permit with the Director of

Immigration Services

Foreign investors with project worth 500,000 USD and above can obtain labour and immigration documents such as work permits, resident permits through the labour and immigration officers stationed at Tanzania Investment Centre One Stop Centre. Click on the blue links bellow for more details.

Obtain Work Permit
   Work permit class A
   Is issued to a foreign investor who is Self-employed (owner of the business, Directors)

   Work permit class B
   Is issued to non-citizen employees who posses prescribed profession including medical and health care professionals, experts in oil and gas, teachers and University Lecturers in Science and Mathematics

CLASS B: Resident permit
This is for all foreign nationals who wish to be employed in Tanzania

   Work permit class C
   Is issued to non-citizen employees who are in possession of such other profession apart from those in category B

CHAPTER FIVE
ABOUT KENYA

Kenya, officially the Republic of Kenya, is a sovereign state in Africa. Its capital and largest city is Nairobi. Kenya lies on the equator with the Indian Ocean to the south-east, Tanzania to the south, Uganda to the west, South Sudan to the north-west, Ethiopia to the north and Somalia to the north-east.

Capital city

Nairobi (Nyrobi meaning 'the place of cool waters' in Maa), is the highest city in East Africa at 1,700 m. Modern and rapidly growing Nairobi has over 4 million inhabitants (estimated).

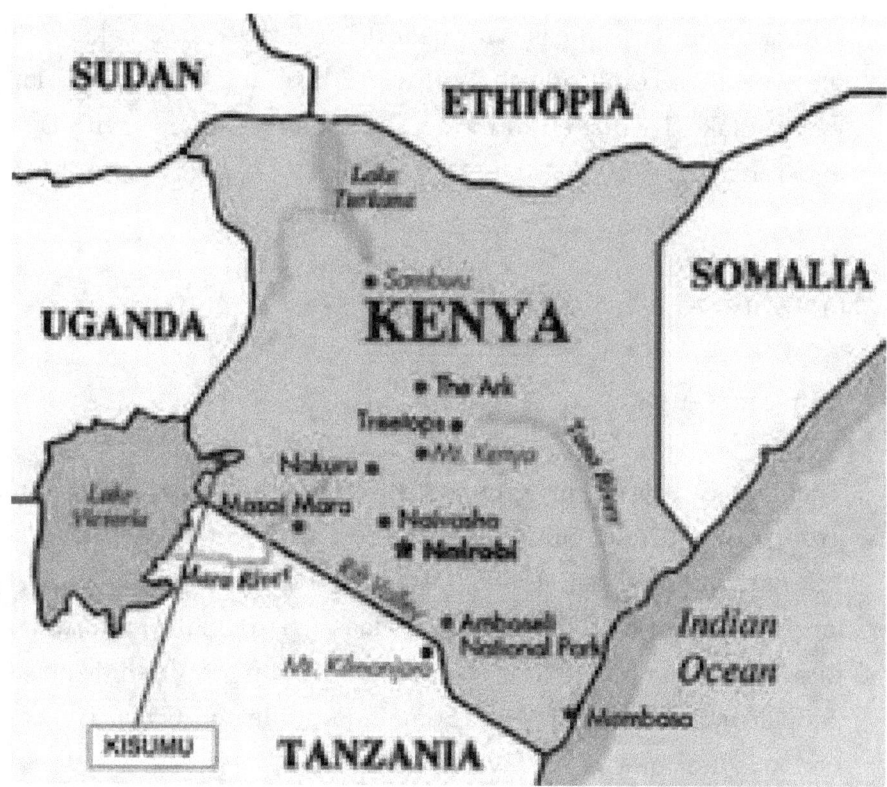

Economy

Kenya is a Lower Middle-Income country and the fifth-largest economy in sub-Saharan Africa. It has a Growth Domestic Product (GDP) of $ 53.3 billion giving GDP per capita of $1,246. In 2014, the economic growth rate was estimated to be 5.3%.

Climate

The country has a warm and humid climate along its Indian Ocean coastline, with wildlife-rich savannah grasslands inland towards the capital. Nairobi has a cool climate that gets colder approaching Mount Kenya, which has three permanently snow-capped peaks. Further inland there is a warm and humid climate around Lake Victoria, and temperate forested and hilly areas in the western region. The northeastern regions along the border with Somalia and Ethiopia are arid and semi-arid areas with near-desert landscapes. Lake Victoria, the world's second largest fresh-water lake and the world's largest tropical lake, is situated to the southwest and is shared with Uganda and Tanzania.

Population
Over 40 million.

Ethnic makeup

There are over 40 ethnic groups distinguished by two major language groups: Bantu and Nilotic. The largest tribes of the Bantu are the Kikuyu, Meru, Gusii, Embu, Akamba, Luyha and Mijikenda. The largest tribes of the Nilotic are the Maasai, Turkana, Samburu, Pokot, Luo and Kalenjin. A third group made up of Cushitic-speaking peoples includes the El-Molo, Somali, Rendille and Galla. The coastal region is the home of the Swahili people.

Religion

Christianity, Hinduism, Sikhism and Islam.

Language

English (official), Kiswahili (official, national), multiple ethnic languages (Bantu, Cushitic and Nilotic language groups). Literacy: 85% of population over age 15 can read and write.
Currency

Kenya shilling (Ksh)

Tourism

Kenya's services sector, which contributes about 61 percent of GDP, is dominated by tourism. The tourism sector has exhibited steady growth in most years since independence and by the late 1980s had become the country's principal source of foreign exchange. Tourists, the largest number from Germany and the United Kingdom, are attracted mainly to the coastal beaches and the game reserves, notably, the expansive East and West Tsavo National Park (20,808 square kilometers (8,034 sq mi)) in the southeast.

Governments and Politics

Kenya is a presidential representative democratic republic. The President is both the head of state and head of government, and of a multi-party system. Executive power is exercised by the government. Legislative power is vested in both the government and the National Assembly or parliamentary lower house. The Judiciary is independent of the executive and the legislature.

Agriculture

The agricultural sector is very critical and has been identified as the engine of prosperity, chiefly due to its direct positive impact on its Kenya's rural population. It contributes approximately 24% of the nation's GDP, 60% of export earnings and about 75 % of industrial raw materials. It also accounts for 65% of the country's total export, 18% and 60% of formal and total employment respectively.

Energy

The largest share of Kenya's electricity supply comes from hydroelectric stations at dams along the upper Tana River, as well as the Turkwel Gorge Dam in the west. A petroleum-fired plant on the coast, geothermal facilities at Olkaria (near Nairobi), and electricity imported from Uganda make up the rest of the supply. Kenya's installed capacity stood at 1,142 megawatts between 2001 and 2003. The state-owned Kenya Electricity Generating Company (KenGen), established in 1997 under the name of Kenya Power Company, handles the generation of electricity, while the Kenya Power and Lighting Company (KPLC), which is slated for privatization, handles transmission and distribution. Shortfalls of electricity occur periodically, when drought reduces water flow. To become energy sufficient, Kenya aims to build a nuclear power plant by 2017.

Landscape

The landscape of Kenya is distinctly divided into two halves – the eastern half which slopes gently to the coral-backed seashore, and the western portion, which rises abruptly through a series of hills and plateaus to the Eastern Rift Valley. West of the Rift is a westward-sloping plateau, and the lowest part is covered by Lake Victoria. The highest point in the country is the snow-capped peak of Mount Kenya (5,199 m), the second highest mountain in Africa. The coastline extends some 536 km from the Tanzanian border in the southeast, to the Somali border in the northeast. The main rivers are the Athi/Galana and the Tana. The major lakes are: Lake Victoria, Turkana, Baringo, Naivasha, Magadi, Jipe, Bogoria, Nakuru and Elementaita.

Flora

Kenya's flora is diverse. Coastal forests contain palm, mangrove, teak, copal and sandalwood trees. Forests of baobab, euphorbia and acacia trees cover the lowlands to an elevation of approximately 915 m. Extensive areas of savannah are interspersed with groves of acacia and papyrus, which characterize the terrain from 915 to 2,745 m above sea level. Bamboo and camphor are common in the dense rainforest of the eastern and southeastern mountain slopes. The alpine zone (above 3,550 m) contains many Senecio and Lobelia plants.

Fauna

There are 80 major animal species ranging from the 'Big Five' (elephant, buffalo, rhinoceros, lion and leopard) to tiny antelopes such as the dik-dik, which is slightly larger than a rabbit. At least 32 endemic species are endangered.

Avifauna

Kenya boasts around 1,137 species of birds. Spotting over 100 bird species in a day is not uncommon.

LIVING AND WORKING IN KENYA

Health

Kenya's hospitals are known for their best health practices, with committed highly skilled doctors and nurses ready to provide excellent health care services to all individuals brought to their attention.

Most lodges and hotels offer resident medical staff and maintain radio or telephone contact with the Flying Doctor Service, which specializes in air evacuations and emergency treatment in East Africa. Temporary membership is available.

Useful places to search:

- Kenyatta National Hospital Government Hospital in

Nairobi
- Nairobi Hospital Private Hospital in Nairobi.
- Aga Khan Hospitals Private Hospital in Nairobi, Kisumu and Mombasa
- M.P. Shah Hospital Private Hospital in Nairobi

Education

Kenya offers a wide range of educational opportunities. There are state run schools (for Kenya Citizens only) and a wide variety of private fee paying private schools.

Useful places to search:

- Kenyan Government department of Education
- Kenya Private Schools Association
- Kenya Secondary School Heads Association
- British Council

Employment and Recognized Qualifications

All Non Kenyan Citizens require a permit to work in Kenya, even for Voluntary work.

Useful places to search:

- Kenyan Government department of Immigration

Entry and residence requirements

For information on entry and residence requirements, contact your local Kenyan Embassy.

Useful places to search:

- Kenyan Government department of Immigration

Benefits

There is no benefits system in Kenya, however if you are working you will be paying in to the National Social Security Fund and the National Hospital Insurance fund.

Useful places to search:

- Kenya Revenue Authority
- National Social Security Fund
- National Health Insurance Fund

Driving Licenses and Vehicles

You can drive on your international driving license for up to 90 days.

Useful places to search:

- Kenya Revenue Authority Kenyan Government department issuing licenses
- Automobile Association of Kenya

Finance

There are many International banks and investment companies operating in Kenya. Below are the basic requirements fo opeing a bank account (may vary slightly with different banks)

Requirements for opening a bank account in Kenya:

- ID or passport
- Minimum opening balance (Varies with different banks)
- Utility bill/ lease agreement(for purpose of verifying physical address)
- Color passport photograph
- Recommendation letter from an employer or other customer

For information on taxation in Kenya: Kenya Revenue Authority

Guidance on bringing medication into Kenya

All Non Kenyans require a permit/visa to live in Kenya.
For Kenya Immigration requirements please visit: Department of Immigration

CHAPTER SIX
THE REASONS TO INVEST IN KENYA

East and Central Africa's Largest Economy

Kenya is the largest and the most advanced economy in East and Central Africa; with strong growth prospects supported by an emerging, urban middle class with an increasing appetite for high-value goods and services.

It is the dominant economy in the East Africa Community, contributing to more than 40% to the region's GDP. The re-based Gross Domestic Product (GDP) places Kenya as the fifth largest economy in Sub-Sahara Africa and ninth in Africa. Although the economy remains small by global standards, it is distinguished from those of most of African countries by the fact that it is one of the most diversified and advance.

Low Risk Investment Environment

Kenya's investment climate is the strongest in the EAC, with FDI flowing in from emerging and developed markets and a high volume of multinationals with regional and continent-wide headquarters in the country.

In 2013, Kenya was the top destination for international investors in the Eastern Africa Region after attracting 12 private equity deals valued at over USD 110.5 million.

Strategic Geographical Location

Kenya's geographical location makes the country ideal for strategic partnerships aimed at improving regional and global market share.

Regional connectivity Kenyan infrastructure is the gateway to the vibrant East and Central Africa region and access to the 138 million population i.e. Mombasa ports, Kenya – Uganda railway.

International connectivity through Jomo Kenyatta International Airport functions as an effective air hub between Africa, Europe and Asia.

Market Access

As well as Kenya's membership to regional economic blocs, coupled with her strategic geographic position, makes the country the gateway to the huge EAC and COMESA regional Markets and beneficiary of several trade preferential arrangements.

Kenya is a member to several trade arrangements and beneficiary to trade- enhancing schemes that include the Africa Growth and Opportunity Act (AGOA), World Trade Organization and EAC-EU Trade Agreement. Soon there will be Tripartite Free Trade Area (FTA) cooperation, a regional bloc of the EAC, COMESA and SADC nations. Potential market: 600 Million people!

Political Stability and Favorable Investment Policy

Empowered by a new constitution and administration, the national and county governments are approaching the private sector as a central partner in the development and growth of the Kenyan economy.

Improving Infrastructure

Kenya's infrastructure landscape is also undergoing significant transformation as evidenced by commitment of over USD20 billion towards infrastructure development through Public Private Partnerships. Infrastructure Strategy: Increasing investment in infrastructure under

PPP arrangements

Reducing Cost of Energy and Improving Energy Availability

Kenya is also perfectly positioned to unleash Africa's power generation capacity through its focus on green and cost effective sources of energy, set to contribute to a 5000MW increase in the national power grid.

Increasing share of power generated from green and more cost effective sources, with a target to increase electricity generation capacity by 5,000MW from the current 1,644MW to 6,700 MW in 40 months.

Large Pool of Labour Force

Kenya prides itself in its large pool of highly educated, skilled and sought after work force in Africa trained from within the country and in institutions round the world. It is estimated that over 55% of the Kenyan population is aged between 15 and 64. This means therefore that majority of the population is active and able to provide labour.

Well Established Private Sector.

Kenya's private sector is very substantial including a number of foreign investors and is touted as one of the most resilient in the world. Key players in voicing private-sector concerns include: Kenya Private Sector Alliance (KEPSA), Federation of Kenya Employers (FKE) and the Kenya Association of Manufacturers (KAM).

Vibrant Capital Markets

Foreign participation in NSE: 54.1% of total equity turnover (January-June 2014)

CHAPTER SEVEN
POTENTIAL AREAS TO INVEST IN KENYA

Opportunities for Investment in Kenya

Many trade and investment opportunities exist today in Kenya, especially in the agriculture, manufacturing and mining industries, as outlined below.

Tourism

Tourism is one of Kenya's leading foreign exchange earner and third largest contributor to the GDP after agriculture and manufacturing. The sector has been growing fast as a result of various factors such as liberalization, persification of tourist markets and continued Government support and commitment to providing an enabling environment, coupled with successful tourism promotion and political stability.

Information & Communications Technology

The size of the local ICT market is estimated at US$ 500 million and it is of note that companies such as Spanco, followed Airtel into Kenya to continue servicing them. These companies are expected to expand into the region , given Kenya's its relative sophistication compared to neighboring markets, and in order to service clients' expansion plans into the EAC and beyond.

Energy & infrastructure

There are investment opportunities in oil and LPG supply and distribution, and in the country's rural electrification and water supply programs. Furthermore, there is huge demand for investment in infrastructure of all kinds, in view of the country's Vision 2030 economic blueprint program.

Banking & Finance

Kenya's financial sector is the largest in the East and Central African region, and it envisions to have a vibrant and globally competitive financial industry that will not only create jobs but also to promote high levels of saving to finance overall investment needs.

Kenyan financial sector comprises of Banking, Insurance, Capital markets, Pension Schemes and Quasi-banking institutions such as: Savings and Credit Cooperative Societies (SACCOs); Microfinance Institutions (MFIs); Building Societies, Kenya Post Office Savings Bank (KPOSB); Development Finance Institutions; (DFIs) and informal financial services such as Rotating Savings and Credit Associations (ROSCAs). Financial intermediation in Kenya has continued to recorded high growth rates due to increased lending as reflected by the rise in domestic credit backed by significant financial innovation.

Sports

Kenya is a sporting nation and renown for prowess in athletics. There is great potential to invest in athletics through setting up centers for training. Investors can help nurture sporting talent from the grassroots level, while also contributing to the development of sporting facilities such as golf courses, car and horse racing etc.

Agriculture

Agriculture is the mainstay of the economy, providing livelihood to approximately 75 % of population. The agricultural sector currently contributes approximately 24% of Gross Domestic Product, generates 60% of the total foreign exchange earnings and provides direct employment to over 311,000 people. The sector has strongly forward and backward linkages providing most of the basic raw material and inputs to local agro-industries.

The major agricultural activities in Kenya are crop production, horticulture, dairy and livestock farming. The principle food crops produced include maize, wheat, beans, potatoes and rice, while major cash crops are coffee, tea, sugarcane, sisal, and pyrethrum. There exists potential in cotton production.

Horticulture

Opportunities exist in production and export of products such as cut flowers, French beans, pineapples, mushrooms, asparagus, mangoes, macadamia nuts, avocados, passion fruits, melons, and carrots. Support services include cold storage facilities and refrigerators for horticultural and other perishable products, seed production, and construction of dams and bore holes, and installation of irrigation systems.

Fisheries

Australian imports from Kenya comprise mainly of fish and related products, and there is room for growth in this area considering the vast fishing potential of the Indian Ocean and Lake Victoria. At present, deep sea fishing, prawn and trout farming are in their infancy but growing rapidly. Opportunity also exists in fish processing (filleting and fish meal production), as well as fisheries-support infrastructure (refrigerated transport, cold storage, etc.

Agro-processing

Numerous investment opportunities exist in this sector. Edible and other oils produced locally include butter, ghee and margarine as well as sunflower, rapeseed, cottonseed, seamen, coconut and corn oil, while a large quantity of palm oil is imported. Investments to develop substitutes for palm oil imports are welcome.

Other opportunities include coffee roasting and grinding, with a further potential such as in the production of decaffeinated coffee for export, manufacture of sprayers and pesticides, and the production and processing of sugar, tea, meat and dairy products.

Poultry Products

Hatcheries for the production of chicken for both domestic and regional consumption are under-exploited.

Leather and Leather Goods

Most hides and skins are processed up to the wet blue stage for export while investment opportunities exist in production of finished leather, offering potential for the manufacture of shoes and other leather products.

Manufacturing

Kenya's manufacturing sector plays an important role in adding value to agricultural output and providing forward and backward linkages, hence accelerating overall growth. The sector now comprises of over 700 established enterprises and directly employs over 200 000 Kenyans. A wide range of opportunities for direct and joint-venture investments exist in the manufacturing sector, including agro-processing, manufacture of garments, assembly of automotive components and electronics, paper, chemicals, pharmaceuticals, metal and engineering products for both domestic and export markets.

Paper products

Kenya has an integrated pulp paper mill plant and paperboard from renewable forest products. However, the country imports coated white lined chipboard and other boards for packaging, newsprint, printed-paper and other type of paper. Investment opportunities exist in the production of paper from other raw material such as bagasse, sisal waste, straw and waste paper.

Textiles and Apparels

Textile, Garment and Apparel manufacturing has a very high potential in Kenya. Sufficient, experienced, productive and inexpensive Labour is locally available, in addition, a well-developed infrastructure, dependable air and sea transport links and support services required by the textile manufacturers are already in place to enhance the development of the industry.

Vehicle Parts and Assembly

The motor vehicle component industry is rapidly developing to supply the needs of a few motor vehicle assemblers to meet certain local content requirements. The plants assemble passenger cars commercial vehicles. Kenya has over 20,000 new registrations annually. Products such as tires, tubes, batteries, springs, radiators, brakes pads, cables, rubber components and filters are now produced locally. A number of firms fabricate bodies for commercial vehicles. A small-scale bicycle assembly venture and a large ship repair operation exist as well. Opportunities exist for manufacture of components for use by local assemblers for domestic market and for export to regional markets.

Electrical Equipment

Investment potential exist for the production of motors, circuit breakers, transformers, switch gears, irrigation pumps, capacitors, insulation tapes, electrical fittings and integrated circuits for both the domestic and export markets.

Plastics, Chemicals and Pharmaceuticals

A large number of pharmaceutical formulations are produced locally in the form of tablets, syrups, capsules, and injectables, but the bulk of pharmaceuticals is imported. There is room for additional investment in the pharmaceutical industry.

Many attractive investment opportunities in chemicals, pharmaceuticals and fertilizers remain unexploited. These include the production of PVC granules from ethyl alcohol; formaldehyde from methanol; melamine and urea; mixing and granulating of fertilizers; cuprous ox chloride for coffee bean disease; caustic soda and chlorine based products; carbon black; activated carbon; precipitated calcium carbonate; textile dyestuff; ink for ball-point pens; and galantine capsules.

Mining and Mineral Products

Kenya has well-developed cement processing plants that satisfy the domestic market and exports to the regional market. Approximately 1.2 million tones of cement are consumed locally each year. The Kenya Mining Industry is dominated by production of non-metallic minerals which are mainly: – soda ash (trona), fluorspar, diatomite, vermiculite, natural carbon dioxide, kaolin, barytes, a variety of gemstones, limestone and lime products including various construction materials. In the case of metallic minerals, some quantities of gold are being produced. Iron ore is produced from localized small deposit and is utilized in the manufacture of cement in the country.

Opportunities exist in the production of glass, as the country is not self-sufficient. A few manufacturing units produce ceramic pottery and tiles, however, substantial quantities of ceramic pottery, tiles, sanitary-ware, and insulators are imported. Investment potential exists in prospecting and mining of other minerals such as gold, precious stones and petroleum.

CHAPTER EIGHT
PROCEDURES TO INVEST IN KENYA

STARTING A BUSINESS

The principal types of business enterprises in Kenya are:

- Registered Companies (Private and Public)
- Branch offices of companies registered outside Kenya
- Partnerships
- Sole Proprietorships; and
- Societies

Company Registration

The Registrar of Companies is responsible for business registrations in Kenya. He/she issues certificates of compliance for foreign companies, certificates of incorporation for local companies and certificates of registration for sole proprietorships and partnerships. Firms must then obtain registration with National Social Security Fund (NSSF), National Hospital Insurance Fund (NHIF) and the Kenya Revenue Authority (KRA). A business permit should also be obtained from the County Government depending on the business type.

New: All company and business registrations (sole proprietorships and partnerships) are being done through the ecitizen online platform but for limited liability partnerships (LLPs) registrations which are still manual and are being done at the company registry.

Starting a local company

A local company is a company incorporated in Kenya. It may take the form of:

- A company limited by shares
- A company limited by guarantee
- Unlimited company

The registration process for the various forms of local company is the same though the requirements and costs vary.

Start a local company (online)

Procedures
1. REGISTER WITH eCitizen

Requirements
1. Identity card
or

Foreign national certificate-alien card
For foreign nationals
or
Passport
For foreigners without alien card.
2. Passport photo (copy)
3. Email address
4. Contact details

Time frame
Attention at counter: Min. 5mn - Max. 10mn

2. APPLY AND PAY FOR COMPANY NAME SEARCH

Costs
Cost detail

KES 100
For a single business name search

KES 50
eCitizen convenience fee

Payment methods: credit cards, Mobile transfers

For payments using cards an additional fee of KES 3.75 is charged.

Time frame
Attention at counter: Min. 5mn - Max. 10mn
Waiting time until next step: Min. 0.5day - Max. 3 days

As time i am writing this book, exchange rate was as follows:

1 USD = 103.3729 KES
1 Dollars = 103.3729 Kenyan Shillings
The USDKES rate as of 21 Apr 2017 at 8:47 AM
Source: http://www.exchangerates.org.uk/Dollars-to-Kenyan-Shillings-currency-conversion-page.html

Additional information
It is advisable to have 3 unique business names to ensure availability.

3. OBTAIN COMPANY NAME RESERVATION

Obtain online here:

https://accounts.ecitizen.go.ke/register-step-1?t=citizen
Time frame
Attention at counter: Min. 5mn - Max. 10mn

Additional information
If you get a rejection it means that your name is already in use or is contrary to public policy and therefore you should reapply using a different name .

4. APPLY AND PAY COMPANY REGISTRATION

Apply online here: https://www.ecitizen.go.ke/

Requirements
1. PIN certificate (copy)
For each director if a local
or

Passport (copy)
If the directors are foreigners showing the biodata page
2. Passport photo (copy)
For each director

COSTS
Cost detail

KES 10,000
For company registration
KES 600
For CR 12 - List of shareholders certificate
KES 50
eCitizen convenience fee

Time frame
Attention at counter: Min. 10mn - Max. 30mn

As time i am writing this book, exchange rate was as follows:

1 USD = 103.3729 KES
1 Dollars = 103.3729 Kenyan Shillings
The USDKES rate as of 21 Apr 2017 at 8:47 AM
Source: http://www.exchangerates.org.uk/Dollars-to-Kenyan-Shillings-currency-conversion-page.html

Additional information
During application, the applicant will key in the name reservation number obtained earlier. Upon completion of the online application, the applicant ought to download the online forms - CR1, CR2, CR8 and the statement of nominal capital and have them signed then upload them in the ecitizen system.

5. SUBMIT SIGNED APPLICATION FORMS

Requirements
1. Signed notice of registered address-CR8 (copy)
Duly signed by the directors
2. Signed company registration form (copy)
Duly signed by the directors
3. Signed memorandum of a company with share capital-CR2 (copy)
Duly signed by the directors
4. Signed statement of nominal capital (copy)
Duly signed by the directors

Time frame
Attention at counter: Min. 5mn - Max. 10mn
Waiting time until next step: Min. 4 days - Max. 10 days

6. OBTAIN COMPANY REGISTRATION DOCUMENTS

Time frame
Attention at counter: Min. 5mn - Max. 10mn

7. APPLY FOR COMPANY PIN

Requirements
1. Certificate of incorporation
2. PIN certificate (copy)
For the directors.

Time frame
Attention at counter: Min. 5mn - Max. 15mn
Waiting time until next step: Min. 5 days - Max. 30 days

Additional information
At least two directors must be on iTax for the application to be successful.

8. OBTAIN COMPANY PIN

Time frame
Attention at counter: Min. 5mn - Max. 10mn

Additional information
At least two directors must be on iTax for the application to be successful.

9. VERIFICATION OF BUSINESS PERMIT APPLICATION FORM

Requirements
1. Business permit application form (original)
2. Certificate of incorporation (copy)

3. Identity card (copy)
Of one of the directors
or
Passport (copy)
Of one of the directors.
4. Company PIN Certificate (copy)

Time frame
Waiting time in queue: Min. 5mn - Max. 10mn
Attention at counter: Min. 5mn - Max. 10mn

Additional information
The applicant ought to have an office or premises in which the company operations will be carried out before one can apply for the business permit

10. ASSESSMENT OF BUSINESS LICENCE FEES

Requirements
1. Business permit application form (original)
2. Certificate of incorporation (copy)
3. Identity card (copy)
4. Company PIN Certificate (copy)

Time frame
Waiting time in queue: Min. 5mn - Max. 10mn
Attention at counter: Min. 5mn - Max. 10mn

11. OBTAIN INVOICE FOR BUSINESS LICENCE FEES

Requirements
1. Approved business permit application form (original)
Time frame

Waiting time in queue: Min. 5mn - Max. 10mn
Attention at counter: Min. 5mn - Max. 10mn

12. PAY FOR LICENCE FEES AND OBTAIN UNIFIED BUSINESS PERMIT

Requirements
1. Permit payment invoice (original)

COSTS
Cost detail

KES 200
For business permit application fees
KES 15,000
For business permit - Fee for a small workshop of up to 5 employees.
KES 4,500
For fire permit license - estimate
KES 4,200
For advertisement license - estimate

Time frame
Waiting time in queue: Min. 15mn - Max. 2h
Attention at counter: Min. 5mn - Max. 10mn

As time i am writing this book, exchange rate was as follows:

1 USD = 103.3729 KES
1 Dollars = 103.3729 Kenyan Shillings
The USDKES rate as of 21 Apr 2017 at 8:47 AM
Source: http://www.exchangerates.org.uk/Dollars-to-Kenyan-Shillings-currency-conversion-page.html

Additional information

All business entities ought to have a trading license and a fire clearance certificate. Entities dealing with consumables must in addition have a health certificate and a food hygiene license. An advertising signage license is applicable for all entities with advertising signage (300mm by 600 mm or less).

13. APPLY FOR NHIF EMPLOYER REGISTRATION

Requirements
1. NHIF employers registration form (3 original)
2. Company PIN Certificate (copy)
3. Certificate of incorporation (copy)

Time frame
Waiting time in queue: Min. 5mn - Max. 10mn
Attention at counter: Min. 5h - Max. 10mn
Waiting time until next step: Min. 1 day - Max. 2 days

Additional information
One can apply for national hospital employer registration at any NHIF branch in the country.

14. OBTAIN NHIF EMPLOYER'S CODE

Time frame
Waiting time in queue: Min. 5mn - Max. 10mn
Attention at counter: Min. 5mn - Max. 10mn

15. APPLY FOR NSSF EMPLOYER REGISTRATION

Requirements
1. NSSF employer's registration form (3 original)
2. Company PIN Certificate (copy)
or
Certificate of incorporation (copy)
or
Unified business permit (copy)

Time frame
Waiting time in queue: Min. 5mn - Max. 10mn
Attention at counter: Min. 5mn - Max. 10mn
Waiting time until next step: Min. 0.5day - Max. 1 day

Additional information
One can apply for employer social security registration at any NSSF branch in the country and the various Huduma centers country wide.

16. OBTAIN NSSF CERTIFICATE OF REGISTRATION

Time frame
Waiting time in queue: Min. 5mn - Max. 10mn
Attention at counter: Min. 5mn - Max. 10mn

Registering a branch of a foreign company

Companies incorporated outside of Kenya can do business in Kenya by registering a branch. The registrar of companies issues a certificate of compliance once all the requirements have been met.
Note:
You can apply online here: https://www.ecitizen.go.ke/

1. REGISTER WITH eCitizen

Requirements
1. Identity card
or
Foreign national certificate-alien card
For foreign nationals
or
Passport
For foreigners without alien card.
2. Passport photo (copy)
3. Email address
4. Contact details

Time frame
Attention at counter: Min. 5mn - Max. 10mn

2. APPLY AND PAY FOR COMPANY NAME SEARCH

COSTS
Cost detail

KES 100
For a single business name search
KES 50
eCitizen convenience fee

Payment methods: credit cards, Mobile transfers
For payments using cards an additional fee of KES 3.75 is charged.

Time frame
Attention at counter: Min. 5mn - Max. 10mn
Waiting time until next step: Min. 0.5day - Max. 3 days
As time i am writing this book, exchange rate was as follows:

1 USD = 103.3729 KES
1 Dollars = 103.3729 Kenyan Shillings
The USDKES rate as of 21 Apr 2017 at 8:47 AM
Source: http://www.exchangerates.org.uk/Dollars-to-Kenyan-Shillings-currency-conversion-page.html

Additional information
It is advisable to have 3 unique business names to ensure availability.

3. OBTAIN COMPANY NAME RESERVATION

Time frame
Attention at counter: Min. 5mn - Max. 10mn

Additional information
If you get a rejection it means that your name is already in use or is contrary to public policy and therefore you should reapply using a different name.

4. APPLY AND PAY FOR BRANCH REGISTRATION

Requirements
1. Certified certificate of incorporation (copy)
Duly certified by a notary public from county of origin
2. Certified Memorandum and articles of association (copy)
Duly certified by a notary public from county of origin
3. Passport (copy)
For each foreign director and the local representative if foreign
4. Passport photo (copy)
For each foreign director and the authorized local representative
For local representative if Kenyan
1. PIN certificate (copy)
2. Identity card (copy)

COSTS
Cost detail

KES 6,800
For registration of branch of a foreign company
KES 50
eCitizen convenience fee

Payment methods: cash

Time frame
Waiting time in queue: Min. 10mn - Max. 15mn
Attention at counter: Min. 5mn - Max. 15mn
Waiting time until next step: Min. 1 day - Max. 2 days

5. SUBMIT SIGNED APPLICATION FORMS

Requirements
1. Application for registration of a foreign company -FC2 (original)
The form should be signed by the applicant
2. Notice of place of business- Form FC4 (original)
It should be duly signed by the applicant
3. Notice specifying opening hours of company -Form FC6 (original)
It should signed by the applicant

Time frame
Attention at counter: Min. 5mn - Max. 10mn
Waiting time until next step: Min. 4 days - Max. 10 days

Additional information
The applicant is supposed to print, sign the FC2, FC4, FC6 forms, scan and upload back into ecitizen portal.

6. OBTAIN CERTIFICATE OF COMPLIANCE

Time frame
Waiting time in queue: Min. 5mn - Max. 10mn
Attention at counter: Min. 5mn - Max. 10mn

7. APPLY FOR COMPANY PIN

Requirements
1. Certificate of compliance
2. PIN certificate Of the directors
3. Contact details

Time frame
Attention at counter: Min. 5mn - Max. 15mn
Waiting time until next step: Min. 1 day - Max. 5 days

Additional information
At least two directors must be on iTax for the application to be successful.

8. OBTAIN COMPANY PIN

Time frame
Attention at counter: Min. 5mn - Max. 10mn

9. VERIFICATION OF BUSINESS PERMIT APPLICATION FORM

Requirements
1. Business permit application form (original)
2. Certificate of incorporation (original + copy)
3. Identity card (copy) Of one of the directors
or
Passport (copy) of one of the directors.
4. Company PIN Certificate (copy)

Time frame
Waiting time in queue: Min. 5mn - Max. 10mn
Attention at counter: Min. 5mn - Max. 10mn

Additional information

The applicant ought to have an office or premises in which the company operations will be carried out before one can apply for the business permit

10. ASSESSMENT OF BUSINESS LICENSE FEES

Requirements
1. Business permit application form (original)
2. Certificate of incorporation (copy)
3. Identity card (copy)
4. Company PIN Certificate (copy)

Time frame
Waiting time in queue: Min. 5mn - Max. 10mn
Attention at counter: Min. 5mn - Max. 10mn

11. OBTAIN INVOICE FOR BUSINESS LICENCE FEES

Requirements
1. Approved business permit application form (original)

Time frame
Waiting time in queue: Min. 5mn - Max. 10mn
Attention at counter: Min. 5mn - Max. 10mn

12. PAY FOR LICENCE FEES AND OBTAIN UNIFIED BUSINESS PERMIT

Requirements
1. Permit payment invoice (original)

COSTS
Cost detail

KES 200

For business permit application fees

KES 15,000

For business permit - Fee for a small workshop of up to 5 employees.

KES 4,500

For fire permit license - estimate

KES 4,200

For advertisement license - estimate

Time frame
Waiting time in queue: Min. 15mn - Max. 2h
Attention at counter: Min. 5mn - Max. 10mn

As time i am writing this book, exchange rate was as follows:

1 USD = 103.3729 KES
1 Dollars = 103.3729 Kenyan Shillings
The USDKES rate as of 21 Apr 2017 at 8:47 AM
Source: http://www.exchangerates.org.uk/Dollars-to-Kenyan-Shillings-currency-conversion-page.html

Additional information
All business entities ought to have a trading license and a fire clearance certificate. Entities dealing with consumables must in addition have a health certificate and a food hygiene license. An advertising signage license is applicable for all entities with advertising signage (300mm by 600 mm or less).

13. APPLY FOR NSSF EMPLOYER REGISTRATION

Requirements
1. NSSF employers' registration form (3 original)
2. Company PIN Certificate (copy)
or
Certificate of compliance (copy)
or
Business permit (3 copies)

Time frame
Waiting time in queue: Min. 5mn - Max. 10mn
Attention at counter: Min. 5mn - Max. 10mn
Waiting time until next step: Min. 0.5day - Max. 1 day

Additional information
One can apply for social security registration at the various Huduma centers in the country or at any NSSF branch country wide

14. OBTAIN NSSF CERTIFICATE OF REGISTRATION

Time frame
Waiting time in queue: Min. 5mn - Max. 10mn
Attention at counter: Min. 5mn - Max. 10mn

15. APPLY FOR NHIF EMPLOYER REGISTRATION

Requirements
1. NHIF employers registration form (3 original)
2. Company PIN Certificate (copy)
3. Certificate of compliance (copy)

Time frame
Waiting time in queue: Min. 5mn - Max. 10mn
Attention at counter: Min. 5h - Max. 10mn
Waiting time until next step: Min. 1 day - Max. 2 days

Additional information
One can apply for national hospital employer registration at any NHIF branch in the country.

16. OBTAIN NHIF EMPLOYER'S CODE

Time frame
Waiting time in queue: Min. 5mn - Max. 10mn
Attention at counter: Min. 5mn - Max. 10mn

Registering a business name (sole proprietor)

Business name (sole proprietorship) is a business structure operated and owned by one person. The owner is the sole decision maker in the business and is liable for all the losses and returns of the business. In most cases it is usually a business structure for small and medium sized enterprises (SMEs).

Note:
You can apply online here: https://www.ecitizen.go.ke/
PROCEDURES

1. REGISTER WITH eCitizen

Requirements
1. Identity card
2. Passport photo (original)
3. Email address
4. Contact details
5. Passport
For foreigners

2. APPLY AND PAY FOR BUSINESS NAME SEARCH

COSTS
Cost detail

KES 100
For a single business name search
KES 50
eCitizen convenience fee
Payment methods: credit cards, Mobile transfers
For payments using cards an additional fee of KES 3.75 is charged.

Time frame
Waiting time until next step: Min. 0.5day - Max. 3 days

As time i am writing this book, exchange rate was as follows:

1 USD = 103.3729 KES
1 Dollars = 103.3729 Kenyan Shillings
The USDKES rate as of 21 Apr 2017 at 8:47 AM
Source: http://www.exchangerates.org.uk/Dollars-to-Kenyan-Shillings-currency-conversion-page.html

Additional information
It is advisable to have 3 unique business names to ensure availability.

3. OBTAIN BUSINESS NAME RESERVATION

Time frame
Attention at counter: Min. 5mn - Max. 10mn

Additional information
If you get a rejection, it means that your name is already in use or is contrary to public policy and you should therefore reapply using a different name.

4. APPLY AND PAY FOR REGISTRATION

COSTS
Cost detail

KES 50
eCitizen convenience fee
KES 800
For business name registration

Time frame
Attention at counter: Min. 10mn - Max. 30mn

Additional information
During application, the applicant will key in the name reservation number obtained earlier.

5. SUBMIT SIGNED STATEMENT OF PARTICULARS

Requirements
1. Signed statement of particulars print out (copy)

Time frame
Waiting time in queue: Min. 5mn - Max. 10mn
Attention at counter: Min. 5mn - Max. 10mn
Waiting time until next step: Min. 3 days - Max. 10 days

6. OBTAIN CERTIFICATE OF REGISTRATION

Time frame
Attention at counter: Min. 5mn - Max. 10mn

7. SUBMIT CERTIFICATE OF REGISTRATION FOR AUTHENTICATION

Requirements
1. Certificate of business registration (copy)

Time frame
Waiting time in queue: Min. 10mn - Max. 30mn
Attention at counter: Min. 5mn - Max. 10mn
Waiting time until next step: Min. 3 days - Max. 5 days

8. OBTAIN AUTHENTICATED CERTIFICATE OF REGISTRATION

Time frame
Waiting time in queue: Min. 10mn - Max. 30mn
Attention at counter: Min. 5mn - Max. 10mn

Registering a Partnership

A partnership is a form of business structure between two or more people who have a common view of making profit. The level of financial risk in partnerships is less when compared to sole proprietors as any loss incurred is shared between all the partners. Since it also involves more than one person's expertise, the chances of the business failing is also reduced. In addition, the formalities of registration (cost, requirements, duration) are minimal making it an attractive business structure.

You can apply online here: https://www.ecitizen.go.ke/

PROCEDURES

1. REGISTER WITH eCitizen

Requirements
1. Identity card
or
Foreign national certificate-alien card
2. Contact details
3. Email address
4. Passport photo (original)

2. APPLY AND PAY FOR BUSINESS NAME SEARCH

COSTS
Cost detail

KES 100
For a single business name search
KES 50
eCitizen convenience fee
Payment methods: credit cards, Mobile transfers
For payments using cards an additional fee of KES 3.75 is charged.

Time frame
Waiting time until next step: Min. 0.5day - Max. 1 day

As time i am writing this book, exchange rate was as follows:

1 USD = 103.3729 KES
1 Dollars = 103.3729 Kenyan Shillings
The USDKES rate as of 21 Apr 2017 at 8:47 AM
Source: http://www.exchangerates.org.uk/Dollars-to-Kenyan-Shillings-currency-conversion-page.html

Additional information
It is advisable to have 3 unique business names to ensure availability.

3. OBTAIN BUSINESS NAME RESERVATION

Time frame
Attention at counter: Min. 5mn - Max. 10mn

Additional information
If you get a rejection, it means that your name is already in use or is contrary to public policy and you should therefore reapply using a different name .

4. APPLY AND PAY FOR REGISTRATION

Requirements
1. PIN certificate (copy)
Of both partners
2. Passport photo (copy)
Of both partners

COSTS
Cost detail

KES 50
eCitizen convenience fee

KES 800
For business name registration

Time frame
Attention at counter: Min. 10mn - Max. 30mn

Additional information
During application, the applicant will key in the name reservation number obtained earlier.

5. SUBMIT SIGNED STATEMENT OF PARTICULARS

Requirements
1. Signed statement of particulars print out (copy)

Time frame
The waiting time for obtaining the certificate of registration depends on the workload at the company's registry.

Waiting time in queue: Min. 5mn - Max. 10mn
Attention at counter: Min. 5mn - Max. 10mn
Waiting time until next step: Min. 10 days - Max. 20 days

6. OBTAIN CERTIFICATE OF REGISTRATION

Time frame
Attention at counter: Min. 5mn - Max. 10mn

Additional information
The online generated certificate of registration is not dully signed and one can collect a signed one from Company Registry - Sheria House, Harambee Avenue P.O Box 30031, Nairobi 00100

7. SUBMIT CERTIFICATE OF REGISTRATION FOR AUTHENTICATION

Requirements
1. Certificate of business registration (copy)

Time frame
Waiting time in queue: Min. 10mn - Max. 20mn
Attention at counter: Min. 5mn - Max. 10mn

Business permit

The various county governments in Kenya are responsible for issuing single business permits to the various business types operating within the counties. The type of business permit to be issued depends on factors such as the geographical location of the business, the number of employees, business type, activities of the business among others.

Unified business permit (Nairobi County)

The unified business permit (previously known as the single business permit) is a permit which consolidates all the licenses required for running a business within the county. It includes: a trading license, a fire clearance certificate, an advertising signage license, health certificate, and a food hygiene license. All business entities ought to have a trading license and a fire clearance certificate. Entities dealing with consumables must in addition have a health certificate and a food hygiene license. An advertising signage license is applicable for all entities with advertising signages (300mm by 600 mm or less). The unified business permit makes it possible for business people to apply for the different licenses in one application without going to the different institutions to obtain them. The permit is valid for one year upon which an applicant ought to apply for renewal.

Obtain unified business permit

PROCEDURES

1. VERIFICATION OF BUSINESS PERMIT APPLICATION FORM

Requirements
1. Business permit application form (original)
2. Certificate of incorporation (copy)
3. Identity card (copy)
Of one of the directors
or Passport (copy)
Of one of the directors.
4. Company PIN Certificate (copy)

Time frame
Waiting time in queue: Min. 5mn - Max. 10mn
Attention at counter: Min. 5mn - Max. 10mn

Additional information
The applicant ought to have an office or premises in which the company operations will be carried out before one can apply for the business permit

2. ASSESSMENT OF BUSINESS LICENSE FEES

Requirements
1. Business permit application form (original)
2. Certificate of incorporation (copy)
3. Identity card (copy)
4. Company PIN Certificate (copy)

Time frame
Waiting time in queue: Min. 5mn - Max. 10mn
Attention at counter: Min. 5mn - Max. 10mn

3. OBTAIN INVOICE FOR BUSINESS LICENCE FEES

Requirements
1. Approved business permit application form (original)

Time frame
Waiting time in queue: Min. 5mn - Max. 10mn
Attention at counter: Min. 5mn - Max. 10mn

4. PAY FOR LICENCE FEES AND OBTAIN UNIFIED BUSINESS PERMIT

Requirements
1. Permit payment invoice (original)

COSTS
Cost detail

KES 200
For business permit application fees
KES 15,000
For business permit - Fee for a small workshop of up to 5 employees.
KES 4,500
For fire permit license - estimate
KES 4,200
For advertisement license - estimate

Time frame
Waiting time in queue: Min. 15mn - Max. 2h

Attention at counter: Min. 5mn - Max. 10mn

As time i am writing this book, exchange rate was as follows:

1 USD = 103.3729 KES
1 Dollars = 103.3729 Kenyan Shillings
The USDKES rate as of 21 Apr 2017 at 8:47 AM
Source: http://www.exchangerates.org.uk/Dollars-to-Kenyan-Shillings-currency-conversion-page.html

Additional information

All business entities ought to have a trading license and a fire clearance certificate. Entities dealing with consumables must in addition have a health certificate and a food hygiene license. An advertising signage license is applicable for all entities with advertising signage (300mm by 600 mm or less).

CHAPTER NINE
ABOUT UGANDA

Uganda is a landlocked country bordered by Kenya in the east, Sudan in the north, Democratic Republic of the Congo in the west, Rwanda in the southwest and Tanzania in the south.

Uganda's total land area is 241,559 sq km. About 37,000 sq km of this area is occupied by open water while the rest is land. The southern part of the country includes a substantial portion of Lake Victoria, which it shares with Kenya and Tanzania.

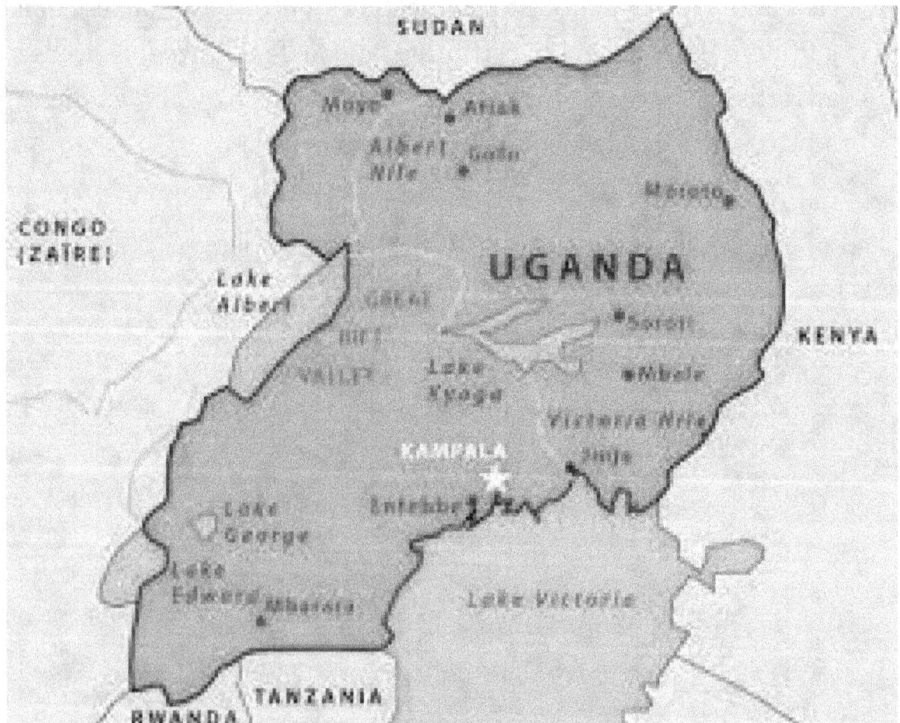

Uganda is located on the East African plateau, averaging about 1,100 meters (3,609 ft) above sea level. The plateau generally slopes downwards towards Sudan explaining the northerly tendency of most river flows in the country. Although generally equatorial, the climate is not uniform since the altitude modifies the climate.

Uganda's elevation, soil types and predominantly warm and wet climate impart a huge agricultural potential to the country. They also explain the country's large variety of forests, grasslands and wildlife reserves. Uganda has a total population of about 32 million people.

Ugandan People

Over 80 per cent of the population live in rural areas and directly survive off the environment and natural resource base.

Population: Uganda's population has continued to grow rapidly over time. It increased from 9.5 million in 1969 to 24.2 million in 2002. Between 1991 and 2002, the population growth rate was 3.2 percent. The population is projected to have increased to 32.9 million by mid 2011

Ethnic groups: Baganda, Banyankole, Bahima, Bakiga, Banyarwanda, Bunyoro, Batoro, Langi, Acholi, Lugbara, Karamojong, Basoga, Bagisu, and others.The Baganda are the largest ethnic group in Uganda and comprise approximately 17% of the population.

Religions: Christian, Muslim, others.

Languages: English (official), Swahili (official), Luganda, and numerous other local languages.

Climate

Uganda's weather conditions are ideal, ranging from the warmth of the lowland areas to the coolness of the highlands in the South West Kigezi.

For most of the year, Uganda is sunny with temperatures rarely rising above 29 degrees. The average temperature is about 26 degrees C, with a maximum of 18-31 degrees and minimum of 15-23 degrees depending on the part of the country.

The rain season is March-May. Light rain season is November and December. Wet seasons are March –May and October-November; dry seasons are December to February and June to August.

Rainfall ranges between 500mm to 2500 mm and the relative humidity is 70 - 100%. The rainfall regime allows two planting and harvesting seasons a year in most parts of the country, without the use of irrigation.
About 34% of the country is covered in wetlands with a dense network of rivers, lakes and swamps.
Generally, the country is endowed with fertile soils. Uganda has some of the largest lakes on the continent including Lake Albert and Lake Victoria

Politics

Uganda is a presidential republic, in which the President of Uganda is both head of State and head of Government; there is a multi-party system. Executive power is exercised by the government. Legislative power is vested in both the government and the National Assembly. The system is based on a democratic parliamentary system with universal suffrage for all citizens over 18 years of age.

In a measure ostensibly designed to reduce sectarian violence, political parties were restricted in their activities from 1986. In the non-party "Movement" system instituted by the current president Yoweri Museveni, political parties continued to exist but could not campaign in elections or field candidates directly (although electoral candidates could belong to political parties). A constitutional referendum cancelled this 19-year ban on multi-party politics in July 2005. General elections are held every five years.

The Government

Type: Republic.

Constitution: it was ratified in July 12, 1995 and promulgated October 8, 1995.

Branches: Executive--president, vice president, prime minister, cabinet. Legislative--parliament. Judicial--Magistrates' Courts, High Court, Court of Appeals (Constitutional Court), Supreme Court.

Political parties: 38 registered parties. Major political parties include the National Resistance Movement (NRM, the ruling party), Forum for a Democratic Change (FDC), Democratic Party (DP), Conservative Party (CP), Justice Forum (JEEMA), and Uganda People's Congress (UPC), among others.

National holiday: Independence Day, October 9.

The 1995 Constitution established Uganda as a republic with executive, legislative, and judicial branches. The constitution provides for an executive president, to be elected every 5 years. President Yoweri Museveni, in power since 1986, was elected in 1996 and reelected in 2001, 2006, and 2011. Legislative responsibility is vested in the parliament; legislative elections are held every 5 years. Because of redistricting, the parliament elected in February 2011 grew from 332 to 375 members, including 112 special seats for women, 10 special seats for military, five for youth, and five for persons with disabilities. The Ugandan judiciary operates as an independent branch of government and consists of the Magistrates Court, the High Court, the Court of Appeal (which also sits as the Constitutional Court when required) and the Supreme Court.

Economy

Since assuming power in early 1986, Museveni's government has taken important steps toward economic rehabilitation and adopted policies that have promoted rapid economic development

Uganda suffered political turmoil and devastating economic drawbacks between 1971 and 1986. This extended period of regression left Uganda as one of the world's poorest countries. Under Museveni's leadership the country initiated a broad range of economic reforms including the notable liberalization of market prices and privatization of public enterprises. These reforms have improved economic performance and sustained economic growth at an average of 7% per annum for the last ten years.

Bank of Uganda

Bank of Uganda (BoU) is the Central Bank of the Republic of Uganda. The primary purpose of the Bank is to foster price stability and a sound financial system. Together with other institutions, it also plays a pivotal role in upholding international best practice in creating a conducive environment for macro-economic stability

Foreign Relations

The Ugandan Government generally seeks good relations with other nations without reference to ideological orientation. Uganda's relations with Rwanda, D.R.C. and Sudan have sometimes been strained because of security concerns. Uganda, D.R.C., Rwanda, and Burundi participated in the U.S.-facilitated Tripartite Plus process, which helped ease tensions and contributed to increased bilateral contacts with the aim of resolving conflicts between the neighbors. Uganda has over 4,000 peacekeepers in Somalia as part of the African Union Mission in Somalia (AMISOM).

Bilateral relations between the United States and Uganda have been good since Museveni assumed power, and the United States welcomed Museveni's efforts to end human rights abuses and to pursue economic reform.

Uganda is a member of the UN, the Commonwealth of States, and several related agencies, and is a founding member of the Organization of African Unity (OAU). It also belongs to the Non-aligned Movement, the Group of 77, and the Organization of the Islamic Conference. Uganda welcomes diplomatic relations with all nations, regardless of ideology.

Uganda is a member of the World Trade Organization (WTO), COMESA, East African Community (EAC)

Tourism

Wondering why it is called 'The Pearl of Africa'? Where else can you see lions prowling across the open savanna as day breaks before white water rafting down the Nile; then the next day set off into the misty mountains in search of the majestic mountain gorillas before settling in to watch a local cultural evening around the camp fire?

Uganda has been ranked the number one destination for tourists for the year 2012 by Lonely Planet which is the largest travel guide and media publisher in the world.

The following week, Qatar Airways, a member of the five star alliances, announced that it would be launching a service to Uganda's international hub, Entebbe Airport.

HOW TO REACH UGANDA

Uganda has become a very accessible destination which can be reached by air or land.

Airlines

Several airlines fly to Uganda, including Aerolink Uganda, British Airways, Brussels Airlines, Egypt Air, Emirates, Ethiopian Airways, Kenya Airways, KLM, Precision Air, Qatar Airways, Rwandair, South African Airways and Turkish Airlines. International flights generally arrive into the modern Entebbe International Airport (EBB) located one hour from the capital of Kampala.

Need help finding flights? Contact one of our Tour Operators in Uganda or one of our International Tour Operators to get assistance with your flights and travel packages.

By Road

There are safe, easy but lengthy bus routes into Kampala from Kenya (Nairobi), Tanzania (Bukoba, Dar es Salaam), Rwanda (Kigali) and Burundi (Bujumbura). The borders with South Sudan and the Democratic Republic of the Congo are more risky - be sure to research the current travel situation as well as visa requirements before attempting travel to or from these countries.

CHAPTER TEN
WHY INVEST IN UGANDA

Investment Climate

- Uganda attained and has had political and social stability since 1986.
- Effective macro-economic policies that maintained economic growth at an average of 6.5% and enabled the country to withstand external economic shocks during the global economic downturn from 2008 to 2011 during which the economy still grew by 3%
- Natural resource rich country (Human and Minerals).
- Totally liberalized foreign exchange regime.
- Consistently improving infrastructures.
- Trainable and fast adaptable workforce from over 30 universities.
- Welcoming population.
- No labour tensions.
- Dedicated Commercial and Industrial courts for quick resolution of business disputes
- A unique multi climate varies from winter on the snow capped Mountain Rwenzori in the west, to the temperate highlands of Western Uganda and tropical forests of the Central region as well as the semi arid North Eastern Uganda. Market access

Market Access through Treaties and Agreements

- The Common Market for Eastern and Southern African (COMESA), a region with a market of about 400 million people in 19 countries.
- The East African Community (EAC) population of over 140

million people.
- Uganda is part of the Free Trade Area of EAC, COMESA and SADC.
- Uganda has a population of 35 million people with a growing middle income class with reasonable expendable income.

Uganda is a signatory to major international investment and business protocols

- Multi – lateral Investment Guarantee Agency (MIGA).
- Overseas Private Investment Corporation (OPIC) of USA
- Convention on the Recognition and Enforcement of Foreign Arbitral Award (CREFAA)
- Islamic Corporation for the Insurance of Investment and Export Credit (ICIEC)
- International Centre for Settlement of Investment Disputes (ICSID)treaties
- Agreement on Trade Related Investment Measures (TRIMS)
- General Agreement of Trade in Services (GATS)
- Agreement on Trade related Aspects of Intellectual Property Rights (TRIPS)
- Duty and quota free access into China (quota free access for over 650 products)
- The USA (AGOA)
- Generalized System of Preferences (GSP) scheme with European Commission
- EU (Everything But Arms) markets.

CHAPTER ELEVEN
BUSINESS OPPORTUNITIES IN UGANDA

Agriculture/Agribusiness

Uganda is among the leading producers of coffee, bananas and oil seed crops (sesame (semis), soybean, sunflower, etc). It is also a major producer of other crops like tea, cotton organic cotton, tobacco, cereals, fresh fruit & vegetables and nuts, essential oils, flowers, poultry, fresh water fish.

Opportunities for investment exist in:

- Commercial farming in both crops and animal industries, as well as aquaculture;
- Value addition (Agro-industries -Agro-food industries;
- Manufacturing of inputs (fertilizers, pesticides etc);
- Cold storage facilities and logistics;
- Farm Machinery manufacturing and assembly;
- Packaging;
- Irrigation Schemes.

The country has been zoned into specific production areas and in order to ease logistics and supply of Agricultural products / source of raw materials, all these areas are well linked to a good national road grid network.

Tourism

The distinctive attraction of Uganda as a tourist destination arises from the variety of its game stock (Including the rare tree climbing lions of Ishasha White Rhinoceros, Gorillas, elephants and its unspoiled scenic beauty including forests hills and Mountain Rivers and lakes. 51% of the world's population of mountain gorillas lives in Uganda.

Uganda is home to 11% of the world's bird's species (a total of 1060 bird species) which offers a wide range of bird species.

The opportunities in tourism range from constructing high quality accommodation facilities, operating tours and travel circuits (bicycle tours, air balloon travel, marine – Lake Victoria and river rafting on the River Nile) to the development of specialized eco and community tourism systems, as well as faith based tourism (pilgrimage to Namugongo – Uganda Martyrs, Mahatma Gandhi Statute and Bishop Hannington landing site on the Nile River).

Mining

Over 80% of the country has been surveyed for mineral quantities and locations. New geo-data shows that Uganda has large under-exploited mineral deposits of gold, oil, high grade tin, tungsten/wolfram, salt, beryllium, cobalt, kaolin, iron-ore, glass sand, vermiculite, phosphates (agricultural fertilizer), Uranium and rare earth elements.

There are also significant quantities of clay and gypsum. Gold occurs in many areas of the country, including Busia in the east, Buhweju and Kigezi in the west, Mubende – Kiboga in the central region and significant occurrences in Karamoja in the north east.

Investment opportunities exist in mining and mineral processing. Uganda provides special incentives to the mining sector with some capital expenditures being written off in full.

The Uganda Mining Act of 2003 and Mining Regulation 2004 grant five types of mining rights.
These include:

> Prospecting License;
> Exploration License;
> Retention License;
> Mining Lease;
> Location License.

Details are available on the website www.energyandminerals.go.ug

Oil and Gas

The discovery of extractable quantities of oil and gas in the Lake Albert region has enhanced the sector's joie de vivre. According to the Petroleum Exploration and Production Department, 21 oil and/or gas discoveries have been made in the country to date. Petroleum laws are in place and a communication desk to disseminate information related to the oil and gas sector was created within the Ministry of Energy and Mineral Development.

Investment opportunities available in middle and down streams in the Sector.

More information on the sector can be got from the Website: www.petroleum.go.ug

Renewable Energy

Uganda has considerable unexploited renewable energy resources for energy production and provision of energy services. The overall Government energy potentialThe goal of Uganda Renewable Energy Policy is to increase the use of modern renewable from below 5% in 2007 to 61% of the total energy consumption by 2017.

Energy Source	Estimated Electrical Potential (MW)
Hydro	2,000
Mini - hydro	200
Solar	200
Bio-mass	1,650
Geothermal	450
Peat	8.00
Total	**5,300**

Source: Electricity Regulatory Authority June 2013

ICT

Uganda's Information and Communication Technology (ICT) sector is one of the most vibrant within the region and fastest growing sector in the economy. This vibrancy hinges largely on the good legal and regulatory frameworks. The supportive investment climate therein has exposed numerous opportunities in ICT innovation services leading to maximum utilization of the existing youthful human resource base as quite suitable for the ICT work.

The newly developed and highly qualitative ICT infrastructure is also ready to accommodate more future investments. Uganda is now connected to three marine fibre optic cables running around African eastern coast in the Indian Ocean.

Uganda is positioning itself to be the hub for Business Processing and Management Outsourcing industry with the region on the Africa's Eastern cost.

Numerous Investment Opportunities exist in the local, Regional and International markets .The largest of the Uganda Business Process

Outsourcing, Information Technology and Information Technology Enabling Services. Industry opportunities are within Agriculture, Health, Tourism, Banks insurance and public administration.

Domestic opportunities have been identified in the areas of:

- Digitalization of services;
- Healthcare services for the ageing;
- Productivity Solutions;
- Web applications;
- Software Development;
- Ware housing;
- Network Integrations

Manufacturing

Uganda's manufacturing sector presents various opportunities in virtually all areas ranging from beverages, leather, tobacco based processing, paper, textiles and garments, pharmaceuticals, fabrication, ceramics, glass, fertilizers, plastic / PVC, assembly of electronic goods, hitech and medical products.

Infrastructure

Although significant efforts have been made to develop and rehabilitate the existing physical and non-physical infrastructure, potential investment opportunities exist in all national grids.

These include;

- Airports and Airdromes;
- Railways Roads and bridges;
- Urban Transport;

- Power Generation;
- Power Transmission
- Power Distribution;
- Water and Sewage;
- Irrigation Schemes.

Financial services

Opportunities for investment exist for international multinational banking groups particularly promoting new or innovative financial products (i.e. Mortgage finance, venture capital, merchant banking and leasing finance) and also micro finance saving institutions, especially to operate in rural areas.

Insurance, in particular, is still a relatively young sector and offers several opportunities for investment.

Education

Uganda runs high quality courses in English at relatively cheaper costs than other education destinations and is dedicated to making investment in the country's knowledge hub a unique experience and a win-win situation for both investors and students.

Investment opportunities therefore exist in Uganda for setting up Public and independent private universities, branch universities and offshore campuses. Other areas of investment include technical & vocational training, distance learning and student financing. Research centers in tropical medicine and medical tourism.

Health

The public health care delivery system in Uganda is organized in tiers, where the Village Health Teams/ Health Centers I, II,III and IV and the General Hospitals form the frontline and primary care, the Regional Referral Hospitals secondary care and the National Referral Hospitals and specialized institutes of cancer and heart, form tertiary care.

The national and regional referral hospitals are semi-autonomous institutions, while the district health services and general hospitals are managed by the local governments. A good percentage of health facilities are privately owned and the private sector provides a recognizable output especially in services delivered.

Uganda has a growing population therefore has increased investment needs in the health sector. While Government and development partners' focus on communicable diseases, there is a need for innovations and private sector participation. This has created investment opportunities in health management, human resource training e-health solutions and logistics, tertiary care services early detection, treatment, medical tourism and manufacturing of affordable equipment and other centers of excellence provide more investment opportunities.

CHAPTER TWELVE
INVESTING PROCEDURES IN UGANDA

STARTING A BUSINESS

Registering a Business Name

- Fill the form of Statement of Particulars required to be given pursuant to the Business Name Registration in case of a firm.
- Hand in the form for a name to check as to the availability of the name.
- The form should indicate the name of the person signing the form against the signature in case of corporate entities being the partners.
- The signature of the endorsee, title and the seal of the corporate entity must be indicated in case of corporate entities being the partners.
- Pay the registration fee and hand in the form at the Business Registry for registration

How to Register a Partnership

- Register a Business Name
- Register a Partnership Deed under the Documents Act Cap 81

Conversion of a Business Name into a company

- File a Notice of Cessation of the Business Name
- Return the original certificate of registration for cancellation
- Go through the procedure for new company registration.

Business Name Registration Fees

ITEM
AMOUNT (UGX)

Cancellation of entry
5000

Certification of business name Certificate
5000

Change of particulars
10,000

Change of address
5,000

Entry on register, ratification or alteration of register
10,000

Notice of cessation
10,000

Filing fees business name statements, documents.
1,000

On application to register a business name.
20,000

Search/inspection fees
2,000

Document Registration Fees

Item
Amount (UGX)
Stamp duty – documents of no monetary value
10,000 per copy
Registration fees
10,000 per first 2 copies of a set of 3 copies of the same document
Search fees
2000
Certification fees
5000 for the first 100 words, and for every folio after the first 100 words ugx   2000
Stamp duty – documents of monetary value
1.5% of the value
Uncertified copy of documents

3000 for the first 100 words and 2000 for every 100 words after the first 100 words.

As time i am writing this book, exchange rate was as follows:

1 USD = 3621.075294 UGX
1 Dollars = 3621.075294 Ugandan Shillings
The USDUGX rate as of 21 Apr 2017 at 8:56 AM
Source: http://www.exchangerates.org.uk/USD-UGX-exchange-rate-history.html

Registration of Documents

REGISTRATION AND CERTIFICATION OF DOCUMENTS

- Present the receipts with the work to the responsible officer
- The responsible officer will do the following

- Receive and record the work
- The client will be issued with the paper acknowledging receipt which shall be signed, state the time the work was received and the personnel who received work and the time upon which the work should be ready for picking

CERTIFICATION OF DOCUMENTS

- Present copies of the documents for certification
- Pay of the certification fees
- Hand in the documents and payment receipt at the Business Registry

Registering a new Company

Company Registration in Uganda is done by The Uganda Registration Services Bureau, an autonomous statutory body established by Chapter 210 Laws of Uganda in 1998. Under Section 4(2) of URSB Act the Bureau is mandated to carry out all registrations required under the relevant laws.

Procedures for Registering Local Companies in Uganda
1. Make an application for reservation of a Name

- Upon payment of the required fee, the suggested name is subjected to a search in the business registry database.
- Once the name passes the similarity, defensive, offensive, desirability test then it is reserved.
- Reservation is valid for 30 days

2. File the required documents for registering a company

a) Memorandum and Articles of association
   The Memorandum of association must state the following:

1. Name of the company
2. Address
3. Object clause
4. Share capital
5. Class, value and number of shares
6. Subscribers, their occupation, postal address and the number of shares subscribed, in case of the company limited by shares
7. Provision for the signature
8. Must be dated and witnessed
9. Where the subscriber to the Memorandum is a corporate entity, the seal of the company be appended

The Articles of Association provide the following information

Sets down the rules that govern the internal management of the company

It must be signed by the subscribers

It must state the subscriber's names, occupation and address

It must be dated and witnessed

b) Company Form A1- Statement of Nominal capital

This form is mandatory at the initial registration of the company

Must state the share capital, number and class of shares, value of the shares

Must be dated and endorsed by the person filing it

Must be witnessed

c) Company Form A2-Declaration of compliance with the requirements of the Companies Act Cap 110

This form is mandatory and it is a requirement that it signed by the declarant, dated and must be witnessed by a Commissioner for oaths

Payment of the necessary fees
- Assessment/payment registration of the necessary or required fee is available at the Business Registry or the client may use the self assessment opinion on the URA portal
- Make payments in the bank
- Present the documents for registration with the receipt
- Registration process begins

Local Company Registration Fees

ITEM
AMOUNT (UGX)

Annual Return Form -first 3 copies per year
50,000

Certification fees-3 copies
20,000

Certification fees - every extra copy after 3 copies
10,000

Company Form A1   N/A

Company Form A2   N/A

Other Company Forms e.g. Forms 3, A3, 4, 7, 8, A9
20,000

Extra copy of Annual Return Form -after the first 3 copies per year.   10,000

Filing fees for amendment of memorandum and articles of association-first 3 copies.   50,000

Filing fees for amendment of memorandum and articles of association- every extra copy after first 3 copies
10,000

Issue of license dispensing with use of word limited company
50,000

Issuance of duplicate certificate of incorporation
25,000

Name Reservation
20,000

Resolution -first 3 copies
20,000

Resolution - every extra copy after the first 3 copies
10,000

Registration Fees for company whose share capital does not exceed UGX 5,000,000/=   50,000

Registration Fees for company whose share capital exceeds UGX 5,000,000/=   1% of nominal share capital

Registration fees on transfer form-first 3 copies
20,000

Registration fees on transfer form- every extra copy after first 3 copies	10,000

Registration Fees on increase in share capital	1% of the increased amount of share capital

Registration fees of any company notice or order to be delivered to Registrar	20,000

Registration of any company application to Registrar	20,000

Search /Inspection Fees	25,000

Stamp Duty -incorporation
0.5% of share capital

Stamp Duty on memorandum & articles of association	35,000

Stamp Duty -Increase in share capital
0.5% of amount by which capital is increased

Registration fees	1% of the amount topped up

Stamp Duty-Transfer of shares forms	1% of the consideration of the transfer.

As time i am writing this book, exchange rate was as follows:

1 USD = 3621.075294 UGX
1 Dollars = 3621.075294 Ugandan Shillings
The USDUGX rate as of 21 Apr 2017 at 8:56 AM
Source: http://www.exchangerates.org.uk/USD-UGX-exchange-rate-history.html

Registration of a Public Company
The procedure is as above however;

- In addition file a Prospectus or Statement in Lieu of Prospectus which must be cleared by the Capital Market Authority

- The Articles of Association will need to specify that the company shall invite the public to subscribe for shares.

Registration of Foreign Companies
These are companies incorporated outside Uganda and are registered in Uganda

The requirements/ procedure are;
- File Memorandum and Articles of Association or any other document certified by the Registrar of Companies the Country of origin
- File a certified copy of the certificate of incorporation
- File company Forms A19,A20,A 21 and A22
- Make the payment of registration fees and hand in the

documentation for processing at the Business Registry.

Foreign Company Fees

ITEM
AMOUNT (U$ /UGX)

Registration of new company constitution/instrument

U$ 250 payable in ugx at URA exchange rate.

Registration Fees for company forms and resolutions-first 3 copies

U$ 55 payable in ugx at URA exchange rate.

Registration Fees for company forms and resolutions- every extra after first 3 copies

U$ 10 payable in ugx at URA exchange rate.

Certification fees- first 3 copies
UGX 20,000

Certification fees- every copy after first 3 copies
UGX 10,000

NOTE:

Registration of Charges Fees

ITEM
UGX

Registration of Charges required to be registered by a company
50,000

Registration of particulars of a series of debentures.
50,000

Registration of receiver/manager of property of a company
25,000

Search/Inspection fees-Register of Charges.
25,000

Company Limited by Guarantee Fees

ITEM
AMOUNT (UGX)

Annual return for -first 3 copies per year
30,000

Extra copy of Annual Return -after the first 3 copies per year.
10,000

Registration fees-for a company with no nominal share capital
80,000

* All other fees are the same as those of company limited by shares

As time i am writing this book, exchange rate was as follows:

1 USD = 3621.075294 UGX
1 Dollars = 3621.075294 Ugandan Shillings
The USDUGX rate as of 21 Apr 2017 at 8:56 AM
Source: http://www.exchangerates.org.uk/USD-UGX-exchange-rate-history.html

References

Macp Online Business, (2014), Business Journal, Procedures, Photographs and images, Dar es Salaam University Press Ltd., Dar es Salaam.

Hornb, A.S. (2010), Small Business Economics, Premier Publishers & Distributors Co. Ltd, Dar es Salaam.

Tanzania Institute of Education, (1996), Business Opportunities in East Africa, Webb, B & Grant, N. (2006), Pearson Education Limited.

Shekighenda, A. T & Durkin J. (2009), International Entrepreneurship & Management Journal, Oxford University Press, Tanzania Ltd.

Quarcoo H. A. M et al. (2008), Procedures of Investing in East Africa, Unimax Macmillan Ltd, Ghana.

Kadeghe, M. (2006), Journal of Business Venturing, Afroplus Industries Ltd, DSM.

Other Africa-based opportunities

http://www.mytopbusinessideas.com/africa/

www.ingramcontent.com/pod-product-compliance
Lightning Source LLC
Chambersburg PA
CBHW081150180526
45170CB00006B/2012